NDE

NEAR-DEATH EXPERIENCES

A GLIMPSE AT WHAT LIES AHEAD

By Francisco Valentín

Copyright

All right reserved in all media. No part of this book may be used or reproduced in any manner without written consent from the author.

I would gladly grant permission provided the reproduction is for educational purposes only once I receive a copy of the proposed material to my satisfaction as to the purpose it will serve.

The unauthorized reproduction or distribution of this copyrighted material is illegal. No part of this book may be scanned, reproduced, photographed or distributed by any means electronically or paper without written permission.

Copyright © 2015 Francisco Valentín

Author: Francisco Valentín

Proofreader: Joyce Frawley

Publisher: Francisco Valentín

TheTranscript.org

TABLE OF CONTENT

CHAPTER 1: THE BIG PICTURE

CHAPTER 2: WHAT AN NDE TRULY IS

CHAPTER 3: MY DEATH EXPERIENCE

CHAPTER 4: DIVINE INTERVENTION

CHAPTER 5: HOW PERCEPTION WORKS

CHAPTER 6: OUT-OF-BODY EXPERIENCES

CHAPTER 7: MAKING SENSE OF IT ALL

CHAPTER 8: LET'S GET LEGAL

CHAPTER 9: LESSONS TO BE LEARNED

CHAPTER 10: THE BEGINNING

CHAPTER 11: FINAL WORDS

To The Reader:

This book renders the chronicles depicting a series of firsthand transcendental experiences, from 1979 to 2011, in a factual and detailed fashion to better explain the relationship of a near-death experience, divine intervention, spiritual communication, and how to understand the subjective nature of the spiritual world through the human mind.

It all started one summer day in 1979, when I barely turned age 18 and due to a fatal car crash, I died. But my death-experience or what many call near-death experience is not what brings me today to public speaking, because that would make me one among many and I'm not an exception to the rule.

Rather, it is what took place on July 7, 2011, when a spirit of light manifested through my son's voice to remind me of an agreement that took place in 1979 in return for my life, which is what makes me come forward before you now—by decree.

Why decree? You may ask. Well, I promise I will fully explain that in chapter 10.

As I disclose these accounts of past events, you will come to realize that what many have termed as a near-death experience is but a glimpse at what lies ahead in a boundless world still unknown to many.

Some believe that a near-death experience is nothing more than a surreal or hallucinatory act of the imagination; others, think it comes from religious reverie, and many theorize it to be a cerebral dysfunction as a result of a life-threatening event.

As it is said: some believe, others think, many theorize, and only a few can attest. I can attest to the existence of that so called surreal world.

Not by conviction, secular believes, scientific theories, cultural background, social discipline or teachings, but by having lived, experienced, and being able to keep the vivid memory of that reality that is so difficult to understand from this plane of reality we live.

I invite you to follow my work as I disclose what has been given to me to help us all remember what we have never really forgotten in the first place, but have kept dormant for so long by focusing on the outside world rather than listening to oneself from within.

You are about to learn from this book what I learned from my death experience back in 1979; how I learned in the year 2000 how divine intervention works when I witnessed my dying mother going through a near-death experience; how I learned how perception works when in 2002 I experienced a near-death myself; how in 2010 a prophecy was given to me and finally, how what had been prophesied in 2010 came to pass on July 7, 2011.

Now find a comfortable, quiet and peaceful place where you can read this book; and get ready to not want to put this book down until the end.

At the end of this book, you will find out why this book is only the first chapter in the life of this conduit, yours truly, Francisco Valentín, who will help you remember Higher Truth, without theological ties, this time around. And remember these words of wisdom moving forward:

There's no mystery in life...only lack of information as to what lies ahead! — Transcript(*)

(*)*Transcript:* Insights of Higher Truth I receive, perceive and transcribe from the (*)*Collective Forces of Knowledge and Wisdom* pertaining to the origin and purpose of life. Five hundred Transcripts in number— and counting!

—Francisco Valentín

DEDICATION

I dedicate this book to the one person who helped me with the proofreading of this book. Her name is *Joyce Frawley.*

Neither one of us is an expert in proofreading or editing material but I have shed my heart and soul while writing this book for the better of humanity and Joyce has gone out of her way to help me proofread the interior of this book in ways that could be best understood.

The beauty lies in the imperfection of this work. So, if you find any grammatical errors, rest assured it is not a careless act but an act of courage while publishing this book in spite our limitations in literary composition.

Chapter 1
The Big Picture

LET'S FACE IT; many of us want to have facts on our side before paying close attention to anyone else's ideas, and what better way other than from a renowned name such as the Gallup Poll for validation?

That being the case, let me crunch some numbers before we move any further. According to a 1992 Gallup Poll, approximately fifteen million Americans have experienced a near-death experience (NDE).

This means that one in twenty people have had an NDE, and written records, validating this, date back as far as the fourth century B.C. by the Greek philosopher, Plato.

The truth is that those numbers don't even come close to the reality of the number of people.

There are thousands of daily cases where those having an NDE dread disclosure for fear of being taken as a lunatic, crazy, silly, fools or even insane.

Many others disregard having gone through the experience themselves by sheer ignorance or thinking it was nothing more than a product of their imagination.

Today there are thousands of written records of NDE's, commonly defined these days as —*the unusual experience taking place on the brink of death and re-encountered by a person after recovery*—as an Out of Body Experience, a vision of a tunnel of light or similar encountered expressions.

The well-known and popular term *near-death experience (NDE)* was coined by Dr. Raymond Moody with the writing of his book *Life after Life*.

In his book, Dr. Moody's intent was not to prove that there is life after death, nor did he think that proof was presently possible at the time of his writings. He just wanted to gather data to study at that point.

He indeed described the event as a phenomenon which he studied, divided and recorded in three categories:

(1) Accounts from persons who were resuscitated

(2) Accounts from persons who in the course of an accident, severe injury or illness, came very close to physical death or

(3) Accounts from people who were told or were present when the phenomenon occurred to others.

The word *near-death experiences* first appeared when Dr. Moody expressly wrote:

During the past few years I had encountered a large number of persons who were involved in what I shall call 'near death experiences.

He arrived at that terminology having learned of those above-mentioned accounts (as unusual experiences that occurred at or near death) or those who had close calls with death as he stated in the *Questions* chapter of his book.

It seems obvious to me that if you died and came back with a story it is because the death process was not fully achieved, therefore, *near-death* would sound more appropriate. But, what would the criteria be to determine that death actually occurred?

To better answer this question, Dr. Moody, broke the meaning of death into three groups:

(1) Death as the absence of clinically detectable vital signs

(2) Death as the absence of brain wave activity or

(3) Death as the irreversible loss of vital organ functions.

Therefore, since there is no way to accurately determine when the point of no return is, he hypothesized that *death is the separation of the mind from the body*.

Moreover, not wanting to take sides against the universally found answer to what death is, Dr. Moody stated: *Some say that death is an annihilation of consciousness; others, say with equal confidence, that death is the passage of the soul or mind into another dimension of reality.*

However, and based upon my personal research and spiritual wisdom, I've found that today it's even more evident of the fact that death is the exiting of the soul from embodiment and the transition of the mind as it goes through a readjusting period before it returns to its original form, which is spiritual in nature.

Furthermore, analyzing the intended word, the term *phenomenon* must then imply the act of returning from (where the experiencer has claimed to have been) which cannot be scientifically proven otherwise.

A few years later, the International Association of Near-Death Studies (IANDS) was founded by John Audette in 1981 based on Dr. Raymond Moody's work.

It was the result of a collaborating effort with Dr. Raymond Moody, Ken Ring and Bruce Greyson, to collect accounts and conduct research on Near Death Experiences. Today IANDS is considered to be the most reliable source of information on NDEs.

On its webpage *iands.org* you will find the most recent definition for a near-death experience.

However, because more and more people are coming forward, IANDS has found itself adding newly defined terms to accounts that won't fit under their definition of a near-death experience, mainly because as research progresses, new findings make the previous terms obsolete unless a new term to accommodate new circumstances is created.

Here is a number of terms that (as of the present) have been added to the list:

Near-Death-Like Experiences (NDLE)

Near-Death-Awareness (NDA)

Death-Bed Observation or Vision (DBO)

Shared-Near-Death-Experience (SNDE) and

Spiritually Transformative Experience (STE)

Let's now take a look at each new definition so you can see what I mean:

Near-Death-Like Experiences (NDLE) is a term used to describe someone who has had a similar experience to a near-death but was nowhere near death.

Near-Death-Awareness (NDA) is a term used to describe if you are a dying person and have had experiences similar to a near-death-experience in one or more occasions before dying.

Death-Bed Observation or Vision (DBO) is a term used to describe if you see deceased loved ones or other beings while dying.

Shared-Near-Death-Experience (SNDE) is a term used to describe if you have felt the emotion of the dying person or experienced what the NDE person must have felt.

Spiritually Transformative Experience (STE) is a term used to describe if you have had a transcendental and inexplicable experience that does not fit in any of the previous categories.

As you can see, new definitions will eventually be added as the research keeps progressing and new experiences are found.

Second in the list in Near-Death studies is the Near Death Experience Research Foundation (NDERF) *nderf.org* founded by Drs. Jeffrey and Jody Long. As of the writing of this book, NDERF is considered to be the largest NDE website in the world with over 4,000 experiences reported in over 23 languages as of the present.

NDERF is devoted to the study of NDE and supportive of those experiencing NDE and related experiences.

Similarly to IANDS, NDERF has found ways to branch itself, by creating independent foundations, such as:

ADCRF (After Death Communication Research Foundation) adcrf.org

OBERF (Out of Body Experience Research Foundation) oberf.org

As I said before, new terms keep arising from different sources related to what kind of experience one has had and the trend keeps growing. Let's take a look at some other terms NDERF, ADCRF and OBERF use to describe similar transcendental experiences:

ADC (After Death Communication)

NELE (Nearing End of Life Events)

DBV (Death Bed Visions)

SOBE (Spontaneous Out of Body Experience)

By now you should be getting my message as you see how terminologies tend to clutter the mind instead of giving clarity.

Other entities, foundations and websites may have come forward today and will do so in the near future; therefore, if I have omitted one or the other, it is not my intent to do so.

By no means am I'm here to disclaim the work that has been done for decades to explain a transcendental experience. In fact, I applaud the work that IANDS and NDERF among others have done with their work to help those troubled by their *inexplicable* experiences with the afterlife.

Furthermore, I praise how these organizations have lead science to take a peek at their work by bringing up the rational study of life after death and keep it afloat.

Rather, my work here is to take you beyond what an NDE truly is and take you even farther by giving you the notion that there *is* a spirit world awaiting us; one that should be understood, without theological ties, this time around.

Therefore, learning what a near-death experience truly is, is one concept that needs to be clarified and well understood before we can move forward to the next lesson.

And for those who may see in me as a religious threat, rest assured I come not to separate but to strengthen your own beliefs by giving clarity to what has been clouded by the intervention and interpretation of those along the way.

Therefore, I shall ask you not to imply, pretend, suggest, or attempt to believe that I ever intend to persuade you in any way against your religious beliefs. My words do not go against any religion nor promote any particular spiritual discipline, but to give clarity to an already confusing world referencing near death experiences.

Having said that, let us start the next chapter explaining what a near death experience truly is.

10

Chapter 2
What A Near-Death Experience Truly Is

THE PREVIOUS CHAPTER was all about history and research to help you fine-tune the subject before going *deeply* into firsthand experiences which is the purpose of this book. Moving forward, I will only speak from my own experiences as I have walked the path for over thirty years after my 1979 death experience.

Therefore, none of what I will be writing moving forward throughout this book comes from what you and I may have read in books, searched over the internet, learned from gurus or masters, taught by secular teachings or read from scriptures from around the world.

See it as a one-on-one conversation between you and me on a lazy afternoon in the park, sitting on a bench overlooking the sunset while listening to my words and reflecting over the true meaning of life.

And for those who don't know me well, throughout my years of personal research, I have become one among the most resourceful, stubborn, hardheaded, inquisitive, logical, and skeptical human beings found on Earth who will not give up until I get a logical answer that can make sense of it all.

So get ready to become inquisitive and follow me very closely and don't let your mind get distracted. My intent throughout this chapter is for you to finally say: I GET IT, I REALY GOT IT THIS TIME!

Now let's move forward. The term *near-death experience* is a coined phrase used to describe a transcendental experience that took place, therefore:

A near-death experience or NDE is nothing more than a glimpse at the spirit world—a glimpse at what lies ahead—a crossover to the other side and back. Simply put: An NDE is a Spiritual Experience to the other side and back, explained by the one experiencing it in ways he or she can only describe. —Transcript

Those having the experience themselves, claim having visited heaven; others, simply call it going to the other side; a few recall being visited by departed loved ones; some, describe the experience as being in paradise; others, claim visiting hell; and in many instances, people claim seeing the light, a doorway, tunnel, or simply hovering over or near them. Those are only a few among many other perceived experiences!

Most of those who have taken a glimpse at the other side, have come back with the impression that they have been deceived all along when confronted with an experience that they never thought possible, based on their scientific, cultural, social or religious believes.

Some became depressed by the uncertainty of what they had experienced; others, became overwhelmed by what they had perceived and could not understand what took place, and only a few truly understood what took place.

Certain individuals may come back with sadness; some return with joy; there are those who feel comfort from what they have experienced, and many erase it out of their memory bank and just move on with their lives. However, these are only a few of the many impressions one returns with after a near-death experience takes place.

I know how it feels when someone tries to explain an NDE and all one hears is a negative response in return. I have read so many distorted answers given by science, and so many others theorizing, philosophizing, pondering, and who knows what else...when in essence, it is nothing more than a glimpse at the spirit world— our true nature, where we all belong and came from...like it or not, believe it or not!

Science seeks for an answer from a neurological point of view. Religion validates it only if certain criteria fits their religious beliefs. Quantum physics indiscriminately embraces all possibilities; and spirituality, needless to say, is so broad nowadays that it needs to be defined first before it all can be considered acceptable.

When asked to describe what a near-death experience is, the Medical field responds with something similar to this: *This could have been a result of a neurological response under these circumstances.*

The Psychiatric field, on the other hand, would probably respond with this statement: *Hallucinations are very common among those who receive physical and/or psychological trauma as in this situation.*

Psychologists would similarly say: *We believe people can see what they want to see, especially when they are in distress, survival mode or after undergoing physical trauma.*

Likewise, the Religious community would most likely claim the following: *This is not in conformity with God's laws, and nothing is said in the scriptures with regard to what is being claimed; for that reason, this does not come from God, and therefore, we dismiss it as fallacy.*

On the other hand, we have another sector I don't want to be left behind: Those are the agnostics who claim not being sure to believe or not and the atheists who declare it to be pure imagination.

Last but not least, there are other, such as the deceivers or trolls who keep writing all kind of stories, theories, and articles simply to keep humanity confused.

I know because I have heard them all; from one-on-one conversations to a lot of what is written over the internet, in books, articles, blogs and video postings. And because I walked that path in 1979 after my death experience, I feel the pain of those who have come forward and ended up being crushed by those claiming to know.

Let's take a look at science to further understand how the human mind works.

As you can see from my previous statement, I can break down science into three categories: General Medicine and Surgery, Psychiatry, and Psychology. All three come from conventional wisdom, which is limited to the idea that if it cannot be seen and if it cannot be duplicated, it does not exist.

To even further prove my point, while searching for a descriptive sentence as to what science is, I found a very interesting one that will better assist you see my point:

Science is a methodical process, which seeks to determine the secrets of the <u>natural world</u> by using the scientific method.

Notice I underlined the word <u>natural world</u> to help you identify the underlying problem: Taking a glimpse at the spirit world defies science, which has not allowed itself to accept the existence of the non-physical world.

From clinical studies to psychiatric evaluations, science keeps theorizing endlessly that NDE's are not Spiritual experiences, without a shred of evidence as to what they hypothesize they are, other than measuring meaningless brain activity, which I will further explain as we deepen into this subject to help you to make sense out of it.

Let me explain why a near death experience is a Spiritual Experience: A spiritual experience is portrayed as a blissful moment of realization, visualization, close encounter, or similar occurrence, upon a crossover between the spiritual and the physical plane.

On the other hand, a near-death experience is known to be when either someone dies or is at the edge of death due to illness or when a bodily injury takes place and the soul, either voluntarily or abruptly detaches from the physical body

In both instances, the indisputable truth is that a crossover takes place (*from the physical to the spiritual*) and what is brought back to memory is then described either as a near-death experience or one of the newer defined terms being used. So continuing, since a crossover to the spiritual world and back is taking place, let's define it as a *Spiritual Experience.*

What in essence takes place most of the time in an NDE is that (§) the soul, which precedes the body, finds itself without the physical body and finds itself in the non-physical realm without a clear memory of its true origin —like it or not, believe it or not!

To go even further to help you better understand what a near-death experience truly is, I have created a video for those who work best through visualization, just as it is said that, *a picture is worth more than one thousand words.*

Please login to my website, look for my video archive, and search for the video title that reads **NDE book cover video**.

However, if you don't have access to the internet and instead choose to learn from this book, let me go ahead and explain the meaning of the front cover of this book in this next paragraph.

Take a close look at the horizontal line across the black board with two end arrowheads. This line represents an imaginary perception of life as linear. Although life is not linear, this is the best way to envision life for this particular purpose only.

See how I've divided this line at the center with a short vertical line dividing the horizontal line into two equal halves.

Notice how I wrote the word PHYSICAL on the right side and SPIRITUAL on the left side. That means that the right side represents *life* in the PHYSICAL world and the left side to the SPIRITUAL world.

Notice how I wrote at the far-right hand side of the board in vertical alignment the word CREATION to denote that the physical world has everything to do with creation.

Notice now how I wrote at the far left of the board in vertical alignment the word ORIGIN to denote that the spiritual world has to do with the origin of life.

Right at the center of these two worlds there is a fine line that you see that separates both worlds.

That fine line is the one someone crosses-over from the physical, takes a glimpse at the spiritual world, and comes back with a memory of what was experienced.

That which takes place in-between these two words is what people call an NDE, but in reality it is no different from a spiritual experience.

Keep in mind this is a visualization exercise and not a true description of an NDE. This image is from my authorship, as it was presented to me in a vision by the *Collective Forces of Knowledge and Wisdom* to help you visualize how a near death experience takes place and to understand that regardless of the experience, what is brought to memory is a glimpse at the other side and brought back through what can only be termed as a spiritual experience.

This drawing was also given to visualize many other aspects of our relationship between the spirit and physical worlds.

For instance, in case you haven't noticed, the graph also attests to the fact that life is one continuous experience either in the spiritual or physical plane. In other words:

Life is one…experiences many. —Transcript

By now you must have a clearer understanding of what a near-death experience truly is. Having said that, please allow me to go back to what I wrote in page seventeen, next to the symbol (§) as it reads the following:

The soul, which precedes the body, finds itself without the physical body and sees itself at the non-physical realm <u>without a clear memory of its true origin.</u>

I want you to pay close attention to these words as I give you an anecdote you will find very interesting to help you understand what I mean by the words *without a clear memory of its true origin.*

Some years ago, when I still resided in my native land of Puerto Rico, I took upon myself the responsibility of caring for a stray female dog I found, who was repeatedly showing up at my doorstep. It was a young female dog around four to five years old.

She seemed helpless as if she had been abused and thrown out of a house, as you may know in times when you see people disposing of their cute puppies when they grow old and they are no longer cute.

My heart went out to her, and I took care of her as if I had her from birth. There was indeed a connection between us both at a spiritual level, and even though I didn't know as much about spiritually then as now, I just felt compelled to help her in any way I could.

Unfortunately, within a year I was called to move to Florida and couldn't take her with me. I desperately looked for a new home for her but couldn't find a helping hand.

In desperation, I went to a shelter but learned that if she was not adopted within a couple of weeks she would be euthanized. That was not an option for me and I literally begged for help at the shelter.

When my words were overheard, a man approached me, asked me for my name and phone number, and told me not to tell anyone, but someone was going to call me and help me out. I followed his instructions and waited for that call. The next day I received the call from a lady who was in charge of a charter program called the *Save a Sato Foundation.*

Her volunteer work was to rescue dogs running loose, in bad shape or in desperate need of a home and send them to the mainland. She wanted to be kept anonymous because if people knew of her work she would be overwhelmed by those who no longer wanted their pets and were seeking an easy way out.

When she saw the dog she told me that the chances of adoption for a fully grown female dog were slim. Nevertheless, she understood my predicament and agreed to help me out.

All she asked in return was a donation since the dog had to be spayed and given all the vet shots before being exported. In appreciation, I complied and gratefully gave her a more than generous donation in gratitude for her help.

Months later, I received a private e-mail with the name of the adoptive party, and I anxiously made contact with them. To my surprise, it turned out to be an elderly couple living in Massachusetts.

The lady thanked me for giving them the gift of *Manchas*; the Spanish name given by my youngest daughter who gave it to the dog for the furry white coat with black spots it had. We kept contacting each other through the years and exchanging photos of *Manchas* from her early stages with us and those most recent moments with them.

Four years later, my son received a chance for an audition at Berkley College of Music, and we all packed our bags to see our beloved *Manchas* as well. When we arrived to see *Manchas* we were all anxious wondering if she would recognize us or not.

Upon our arrival, we greeted the lovely couple who adopted *Manchas*, but between greeting them and seeing *Manchas* again, we all got confused as to who we should greet first.

My youngest daughter, who was merely seven when she last saw *Manchas*, happens to be very emotional, couldn't contain her tears and went straight to *Manchas*. What I unfolded is the reason for this story being told.

Manchas barely recognized us. At first, she barked at us and didn't wag her tail in a welcoming fashion. When my daughter approached her in tears, *Manchas* got confused, apprehensive, and you could tell she had mixed emotions because, it seemed she could not recall who we were or what was happening.

When I approached her, I thought that since I took the most care of her, she would most likely recognize me, but I got the same reaction.

Alternatively, I approached her knowing she must recognize the particular way I caressed her neck in a unique way that only she knew, but she held tight to her new family. I knew she was definitely feeling something, but I also knew she couldn't make sense of those feelings.

As the hours went by, we shared stories with *Manchas*' new family, and I noticed *Manchas*' persistent confusion. I could feel she wanted to approach me, but something wasn't making sense to her. Something was wrong, and driven by instinct, she kept her distance.

The attachment she grew with her new family made our presence an uncomfortable one, and was making me feel uncomfortable as well.

By the time we were ready to leave, I could see how *Manchas* looked at me, as if not knowing if I was real or not. It broke my heart knowing how difficult it must have been for her seeing me again, yet not knowing if I was who she thought I was and what to do about it.

But, after having seen her new family and how they pampered her with so many toys, giving her a life of caring and cuddling, even seeing how they treated her as if she were one of the grandkids, it was enough for me and I left that home with a smile on my face.

—End of story.

This is what happens to your soul when it detaches from the physical body; for your soul having lived for so long in this physical world, can no longer relate to the etheric realm (where it once dwelled), and therefore, confusion, denial, disturbance, anxiety, apprehension, or even the process of non-acceptance takes hold of your thought process. I know how it must feel because I was there too, back in 1979, when I found myself without a physical body to identify myself with.

The soul's experience under an NDE (*spiritual experience*) resembles much of the behavior of *Manchas* when she could not identify the sudden reality she was experiencing by being visited by some strangers she somehow paradoxically knew!

What differentiates the term NDE from what is commonly known as a spiritual experience is that an NDE makes reference to the soul detaching in a sudden or uncontrolled fashion, while a spiritual experience is said to occur while in dreams, subtle awakening, meditative state, or a non-life-threatening event. Make sense now?

There is much more to be explained in order for you to make sense of all of this, but for now let's move along one lesson at a time.

Lessons to be learned:

§ A near-death experience is nothing more than a spiritual experience on its own.

§ An NDE, OBE, STE and many other connotations given by men to these experiences are nothing other than spiritual experiences as a whole.

My message to you:

Most of those who have taken a glimpse at the other side and have come back claim they didn't want to come back to the physical plane while in the spirit world. Do they know something we don't?

Chapter 3
My Death Experience

ONE SUMMER DAY in 1979, I was traveling with my closest friends to *El Yunque Natural Forest* in my native land of Puerto Rico. That day was glorious; and it was going to be the last summer my friends and I would spend together before going our separate ways to college.

We were six teenagers cruising in separate cars. I drove my car with my best friend, and the other four in another car were following closely.

A curious detail I must add is that on that particular morning, my mother was unusually reluctant to let me go, but didn't hold me back, so I was free to go.

Once we arrived at our destination, we took off with all our gear and headed for a long uphill walk through alternate steep and less steep trails for hours.

Reaching the peak of a mountain at over 4,000 feet above sea level was the most enticing part of the journey and because of our youth, we had the strength to climb non-stop just to have lunch at the mountain's peak— and we did!

At 4,000 feet, we could all see our beautiful island's coast at an almost 360-degree panorama. Needless to say, the view was spectacular! Nature was all around us, and the feeling was indescribable as we descended just past midday with feelings of joy and harmony.

While driving back home, we were having fun exchanging silly conversations from one car to the other with a set of walkie-talkies that one of my friends had brought. Keep in mind the year was 1979, and carrying walkie-talkies in those days was like giving an eight-year-old his first mobile device in today's frame of reference.

It was a Sunday. We knew heavy traffic was going to start setting in past 4PM; and because we wanted to beat the bumper-to-bumper stop and go heavy traffic, we increased speed to avoid the expected traffic congestion near one particular area miles away.

As we began to increase speed, it slipped my mind that during the week I had gotten a rear flat tire and was running on my spare tire which happened to be a nylon-belted spare tire (something common in those days), compared to the other three steel-belted tires making me vulnerable to lose traction under adverse conditions.

Suddenly it happened—as I attempted to change lanes my car hit a water puddle, swerved, and I lost total control of my car.

All I remember was a flash of memory of looking at my friend's car, as I cut in front of them diagonally, at full speed, and headed towards the median.

I immediately heard a loud banging noise when the car frame hit and jumped the median heading towards the opposite lane.

The next thing I remember was a second memory flash when I had invaded the opposite lane and was headed towards what I recognized as a full size Chevrolet Monte Carlo and making split-second eye contact with the driver before impacting driver-side-to-driver-side in the opposite direction at full speed.

The impact was such that the full-size car made my flimsy Datsun B-210 spin several times ending in a dead stop.

What I don't recall and what witnesses saw as the scariest moment of all, was when my car stopped spinning and a second car impacted me on the driver's side at full speed…and everything went blank.

What you're about to read is the actual monolog I vividly recall having while disembodied in a realm I barely knew.

MONOLOG OF MY SOUL:

—Where am I?

—*What just happened?*

—*Why is it so dark in here?*

—*I hear no sound!*

—*I see no one.*

—*Why am I suspended in mid air?*

(time elapsed)

—*I can see a dim light… far away. I cannot make it out… but I see it is approaching.*

—*There must be someone behind that light!*

—*Yes, there's a kind-of-figure or someone… but now the light is all around me…it's swirling!*

—*But wait…it's not one…but many!*

—*They are all swirling around me!*

—*It feels like they are all creating this swirl around me!*

—*What is this feeling that feels so good?*

—Oh! Peace, that's what they are giving me, peace.

—I'm trying to see what they look like, but can't make any of it out.

—I can't put a face, but I can see they are beings... I know they are beings!

—I can feel their essence, but I can't figure out what they are or what they look like.

—Let me focus on one.

—It's out of focus, but I can see...it looks translucent, like a... can't really tell.

—They are all making this swirl of light around me!

—Whatever they are, they are just giving me their peace, like bathing me with it, or whatever it is, to make me feel just in peace.

—They want me to stay calm; I know they want me to stay still, but why?

—It feels so good I wouldn't mind!

   (time elapses)

—Someone is approaching!

—It feels as if someone is getting closer.

—It's overpowering everything!

—What is this presence?

—OH! It's so powerful yet so gentle.

—It's a bright light that seems to come from everywhere.

—It is overshadowing everything! And getting closer! But it feels good.

—Wow! It's so powerful. Is this why they wanted me to stay still?

—Is this what they want me to see?

—I can't believe how powerful this force is...and it feels good!

—Let me ask, I need to ask.

— Who am I? Who's my mother? Who's my father?

—It's not answering. Why is it not answering?

—Why am I not getting an answer?

—Oh no! There's something wrong...I feel pain!

—Why am I feeling pain? What have I done wrong?

—I've stayed still; I'm just waiting for an answer!

—Why am I feeling pain all of a sudden? Where is this pain coming from?

—No, I don't want to go back. I want to stay here! I don't want to go!

—It's hurting, oh! it hurts-so-much!

—Where am I being taken?

—Feels like a tunnel...a long tunnel...and it is getting narrower and narrower!

—What's happening?

—I want to go back where I was, please take me back...take me back!

That's when I opened my eyes as I was being pulled out of my car as a result of the near-fatal car wreck I was involved in.

THE EXPERIENCE:

I couldn't get back to that *place* as hard as I tried. However, I can still recall the experience after over thirty-five years. I kept it in living memory as if it had taken place last night.

It was *emptiness* as never experienced before. You may call it total darkness...If you will. It felt like a place, but I instinctively knew it was not a place; it was something different.

It was simply where everything begins and is only perceived as total darkness, because there's no other way *our* brain can define such a term for the emptiness I experienced.

It was a place with no boundaries and where a physical body does not exist. I call it *the void*. Not the void everyone knows as we look up into the cosmos that belongs to the physical world; but the *void* I am making reference to is the very much existent void that belongs to the non-physical plane of reality, better known as *the spirit world.*

The void is believed to be nothingness, but in essence the void is that space, unknown and unreachable by men; for, to be there you must not have a physical body, because the void belongs to the spiritual world.

The *void is* where everything begins and where it all ends. The void is like the empty space you know that serves to hold matter in place; but, it belongs to another realm.

While in the void, I felt the most inexplicable feeling of *peace*. Some call it love, but I would rather define it as peace. Love needs someone or something in order to be expressed, but peace needs no one but yourself and is experienced from within.

I felt peace, as I have never experienced it before, yet I was able to recognize it because it felt familiar to me. Imagine being released from all your earth-bound responsibilities, worries, errands, chores, including the responsibility of having to breathe, having to eat, walk, or even having to go to sleep. Imagine not thinking of the past or future, but just living the moment.

That's as close as I can get when it comes to analogies to help you understand what peace felt like. But don't be confused thinking that peace is precisely as everything I have described before, because, an analogy only brings you a little closer to what cannot be described with words.

It's like a language that we don't speak; something we cannot describe, because there are no words to describe it and no reference point to start with.

The closest I can take you to true peace is by taking you into a meditative state and not allowing thoughts to cross your mind. If you ever achieve that state of mind, then you will be close, but not close enough to the peace that is felt on the *other side*— where we all have lived.

I can only describe the void as emptiness, total darkness (as we know it) yet it was full of life.

However, be careful with my choice of words. I'm not describing a life full of trees and animals, surrounded by people, with places to go, or pathways to travel and so forth. I am describing that which cannot be described.

It's like the air that you breathe, that even though you cannot see or hold it, you know it gives you life as you breathe it.

It is a life as pure as I can describe it; and it is where you can just stay still and breathe (metaphorically speaking) life in the etheric world.

I then realized, I was something or someone but couldn't make sense of whom or what I was. I couldn't see myself, but I knew it was me: I knew I was myself.

It's a bit hard to explain, but let's say it felt as if I never knew there was such a thing as a physical body.

I just instinctively knew my true nature and that I was! No physical body and no place to dwell, but one mind thinking of itself. Now that I think of it, it felt amazing!

Although I was baffled by these new discoveries, one thing I knew for sure—*I was still myself!* It was me all along! I was not in a physical body, nor was I in a place to dwell. *That* I knew for sure and without reservation: I was still myself.

If nothing in this book resonates with you and only the following sentence stays in your mind for years to come, I would have accomplished my mission by delivering my whole message regardless of how many pages this book may have:

When you cross over to the other side—YOU WILL STILL BE YOU!

It is hard to explain, but I was unable to identify with the one who responded to the name Francisco Valentin; nor, did I have a gender or a physical body.

I had no point of reference as to whom I was or had been, but, I did know at that very moment, (without a shadow of doubt, since I lived the experience with total clarity and without theological ties), that *I simply was*—period.

Although I couldn't respond to a physical body or identify myself with one, I knew my essence was all I needed, as I was myself all along.

While in the void I was not alone. I could not only feel life around me but I could also see it! I already knew that I didn't have a physical body, but somehow, I could see. Not with the physical eyes that can see images from the material world, but I knew I had some kind of vision.

Somehow, I knew my mind (not the brain) was registering this new environment in ways I never thought possible.

It was a vision that had no colors. Just reflections, or glimpses (like night vision) powerful enough to allow me to perceive the presence of what I may describe as *beings* that up until now I still can't literally define.

I was surrounded by their presence. I could only describe their presence as if I was receiving their peace. It felt so incredibly peaceful that I couldn't and still can't find words to describe it.

What I saw I could not responsibly describe as angels, archangels, ghosts, spirits, loved ones or any of the thousands of claims I've heard attributed to this scenario during my entire lifetime.

I knew, from the moment I saw them, their true nature and not to attach what I saw to any pre-conceived ideas I had already learned; much as if I was being prompted to see but without theological ties.

Let me take this moment to give you a brief understanding of the belief system I was indoctrinated to believe.

I was born and raised as a Catholic. I attended the most prestigious Catholic Private School in Puerto Rico still to this day—Colegio San Ignacio de Loyola.

I attended mass every Sunday as part of my curriculum; not to mention, I also studied Catholicism as part of my daily academic program, therefore, I should have known what an Angel was.

But reality struck when what I *saw* and perceived (while in the void) did not fit any of what I had studied and learned as to how heaven or purgatory should have looked.

I was in awe, not for what I saw, but for what I didn't see. It was a moment of truth, as I was unveiling the true nature of that world which was completely different from what had been taught to me since childhood.

What I am about to describe is not a metaphor, but instead, what I saw as perception, which took place in the human mind, as it brought the experience back to memory.

The closest I can explain it is as if I could only see the vibration that emanated from *them* as they gave me peace when I found myself in the midst of a swirl of white clouds while suspended in mid-air.

Please allow me to explain here how *perception* works for later on throughout this book.

There was no spoken communication because it wasn't needed. Their presence alone gave me comfort, like being bathed in love, but a love that could not be described but felt beyond any known definition of what I knew love to be.

Some may call it *bliss*, but even that word bliss, falls short when it is experienced in the physical world. This love or bliss, that I would rather call *peace*, goes beyond human comprehension; and I have felt every bit of it deep inside me ever since, to this day: What has been known cannot become unknown!

Then the unexpected happened: Suddenly but subtly, I became aware of another presence that overpowered the love and peace I was being surrounded with.

I noticed that there was an overwhelmingly powerful presence, without boundaries, spreading around everything that surrounded me.

At first, I didn't know what it was, but as it approached I knew what it was, but it had no physical presence. It was something I couldn't see, but intensely felt.

And I couldn't call it by name because it was not in conformity with what I had been told it to be.

It was beyond my reasoning ability and was not confined to an image, hierarchy, or creed.

Notice that my words are making reference to an *it* and not to *Him*. To ease your mind—*it* was the presence of God; but, not the God I had been conditioned to visualize, but a God who has an energy force which can easily be wrongly transmuted as a father figure, a Master, a Ruler, or The Almighty Powerful Supreme Being that must be feared and rules everything that is and exists.

By explaining this concept, I want to make sure I'm not misinterpreted by my choice of words, therefore, let me explain why I call it *the presence of God* and not God as Himself or itself. It was a *presence* because it was the acknowledgement of an existence, but not of a God in physical or spiritual form as many claim.

This presence gave me comfort knowing there is something far greater than what I had been taught that existed, and I knew this presence because I remember having experienced it before…many times.

And this presence's greatness extends to all there is and exists, with ramifications in us, diversified in us all, branched in all there is and exists, ever expanding, as creation takes place, infinitely:

For there is a beginning and an uncertain end, and it's presence IS the beginning and the end as well.

WHAT I'VE LEARNED:

Paradoxically as it may seem, it all made sense! It was so clear and easy to understand! But what I knew, I couldn't explain it, because I was too young to comprehend it.

But it was all in memory so I could explain it when the time came, as I'm doing here right now. Let me portray a one-sentence story for you to see what I mean by the sentence you just read:

Once a child was told what life is all about, but the child knew not what those words meant, until the day he had to live life on his own to then realize what those words meant. —Transcript

Today, I understand what I learned back in 1979, but couldn't comprehend then. Had it not been for the reminder that took place in 2011, I would not have fully understand what took place while I was in the void.

The facts remain the same, but its magnitude is something that was beyond reach!

I never would have unveiled the truth that lies behind what a near death experience truly is, otherwise.

Today, I know I am a soul and what death is (and what it is not); where I was; who those beings were; what God is, and most importantly, today, I know who I am, where I came from and what my purpose is in life!

I invite you to follow my work so you can also know who you truly are, where you came from and what your true purpose is in life. Everyone has one. It's just that we have forgotten it a long time ago, and it is time to be reminded once again!

And if **you** fear death, or if **you** fear an illness, pain, suffering or the uncertainty that brings death, **STOP.**

When I was in the void, I had no memory as to how I got there. I had no pain or reminiscences of the fear I must have endured at the scene of the accident or afterward.

I didn't know what had happened and had no grief, remorse, resentment, worries or such. Peace was all I felt (and so will you,) for as long as you do the right things in life. But please allow me to further elaborate on this in Chapter 9.

While in *the void* I asked myself three questions:

—*Who am I?*

—*Who is my mother?*

—*Who is my father?*

But I received no answer. I swiftly knew those answers had to come from within, but I was clueless as to how to retrieve the answers.

All I know today, is that there is a hidden space in my memory bank leading me to realize that there is more than what I was allowed to bring back to memory.

Today I know, deep in my soul, that there is much more information stored away to be revealed at the right moment.

Just as in the (*)reincarnation process where one becomes disconnected from knowledge, so one can do one's deeds without predisposition or judgment.

(*)Reincarnation: The evolutionary process of the soul not yet fully understood by men, discarded by many, but essential to our spiritual growth. Once fully understood, life begins to make sense. —Transcript

THE RETURN:

While in the void, I began to feel excruciating pain as if my insides were being ripped apart. I felt as if I was being sucked into a funnel shape in the void going to a narrow and narrower place.

It was as if I was turning from a juicy grape into a raisin in seconds. Out of all the experiences that I can recall, this one was the most fearful moment of all. The pain was unbearable.

Not knowing what was happening, I was simply returning to my physical body and "plugging" into my nervous system. All I could think of was the astronomical amount of pain I was bearing. It felt as if every cell in my body was screaming in pain.

The pain was such that my brain couldn't register the intensity that I was being subjected to. And the instant I felt someone touching me, I felt like a thousand volts were discharged into me. I immediately regained consciousness, opened my eyes, and the first thing I saw was the right edge of my car's windshield as I was being rescued from my car from the passenger side.

I instantly knew I was fully conscious in the physical world and no longer was where I had been. I was still myself, but had returned to the physical plane.

I was conscious enough to know that I was being pulled out of my wrecked car and felt how I was laid on the grass waiting for assistance. I began to recognize my environment knowing that what I had previously experienced had nothing to do with the physical world where I had just returned.

I knew that where I had just come from I was free, but here I was in pain and bound to a physical body that I no longer wanted to inhabit.

As I lay on the grass, I gradually became more familiar with my surroundings. I could see flashing lights, and cars passing by with their headlights on. I could smell the exhaust fumes from the piled-up cars and traffic the accident had created.

I could hear noises from all over and felt the presence of people all around me. I even remember someone shouting at the crowd to stay away and give me room to breathe.

I could see, hear, smell and feel…especially pain. By now I was testing my physical senses one by one. At first, I attempted to feel my left hand and was able to move it even as much as it hurt. I moved each one of my fingers, and tested the intensity of the pain to see if I had any broken bones.

Little by little I moved each joint and extremity just enough to know if it was still there, until I reached my legs. I couldn't move either one. I freaked out but I was too weak to move them and by then the pain was so intense that I was about to faint.

Needless to say, I fell unconscious as my body kept shutting down due to the severity of pain it was bearing. I knew when I was conscious or when I was unconscious because I clearly remember the big difference between being unconscious and being on the other side. It was something I knew but could not explain.

While lying down I kept taking in all that was happening. I knew where I was, but also knew where I had come from; and I just wanted to go back! That's all I wanted: To go back...to go back home.

I had no way of knowing why I came back. Besides, even if I knew I had no way of knowing how to handle it because I was too young to comprehend what I had experienced.

But because one doesn't get to remember those agreements when one incarnates, I had to do what I came back to do and do it unknowingly, in compliance with the agreement that later was revealed to me in 2011 *(previously explained under 'Note to the Reader.')*

From that point on, I was in and out of physical consciousness only remembering glimpses of what was happening around me. The accident took place around 4 PM, but by the time I was rescued from my car it was already dusk.

Being close to the equator in the Caribbean, and taking into consideration that it was a summer day, it must have been close to 6 PM by the time I was pulled out of the car and laid on the grass.

Two long hours had gone by from the time of the impact to the actual rescue. What could have happened during those two long hours, when it only felt as a few minutes that I was in the void?

Could I have been in another dimension where time runs differently? How much can you reflect on in two hours, which only felt like minutes?

I know that these days there are many philosophers and theorists claiming that time does not exist on the other side.

Let me ask you then, if you are playing ball for one hour and it seemed like minutes, is it because you were living life much faster than Earth's rotation time?

And if you fear for your life for one minute and it seemed like an hour, is it because you were living life much slower than Earth's rotation time?

The answer is none of the above. <u>Time does exist</u>, but is subjective to your state of being. *As long as there is movement, there is time.* If you ever wonder if time does exist on the other side, the answer is <u>YES</u>, it does; not as we know it but yes it does exist. Let me explain:

I recall transitional moments throughout my experience on the other side. First, I found myself in the void; second, I saw what you may call spirits; third, I felt the presence of what many term as God; fourth, I asked myself three questions; and fifth, I knew when I returned.

It took me five steps, five experiences, five separate impressions in my consciousness, five registers, to validate it. Therefore, time does exist; time is movement, and while in the void I moved, therefore, time does exist—not how we know it, but it does exist.

Time is movement measured in any given form. Therefore, if I was bathed in love by beings that were swirling around me, then such manifestations represent a cycle by its movement. However, it's not the same time measured by Earth, because it's not reigned by the physical but by the spiritual world.

If you ask me, I could only describe it as *enough time to know that time does exists.*

RE-ENACTING THE SCENE OF THE ACCIDENT:

Although I have been giving you bits and pieces of the car wreck, let me now reconstruct the scene of the accident from my own memory and from what I gathered from my witnesses, in chronological order, so you can have a clear picture of this catastrophic event.

One Sunday summer day in 1979, I was driving westbound on PR interstate road #3 somewhere near the town of Canóvanas, Puerto Rico. I was driving my 1976 white Datsun B-210 returning from a long beautiful day of a mountain hiking adventure.

It was around 4 PM when I lost control of my vehicle, jumped the median, and landed in the eastbound (opposite) lane, as I briefly explained at the beginning of this chapter.

Witnesses said that as I hit the median, my car catapulted and landed in the opposite lane racing toward the oncoming traffic. The impact from jumping the median blurred my mind and my foot froze on the accelerator.

As the car hit the ground I raced at full speed towards a Chevrolet Monte Carlo (twice my car size and twice my car's curb weight).

My passenger friend later told me he saw me freeze and in a fraction of a second, he grabbed the steering wheel with his left hand and yanked it towards the right to avoid a head-on collision.

It all happened so fast that what could have turned into a head-on collision became a driver to driver side-wipe.

I will never forget the look on the other driver's face when our eyes met as both cars side-wiped at impact.

But because of the speed and the impact force, his 2-ton car's front end smashed into my barely 1,700 lbs. car's left rear axle and made me spin before reaching a full stop transversely to the oncoming traffic.

I was still safe and alive for one last second of my life when the unexpected happened:

Witnesses claim that the driver of an oncoming car heading towards me froze and raced at full speed side-impacting me at over 50 mph to my fatal death.

To give you a point of reference, the impact was so severe that my driver's door panel was crushed against the center console and taking me with it.

I received the full impact of a mighty force that could only be described by the image that follows—next page.

From this image, you can clearly see how my survival defies all physics as to how a young man with a 5'9" build and barely 125 lbs. of body weight could have survived a 50+ mph impact into the side of this flimsy car.

From what I was told, my friends driving the other car rushed to where my car landed but couldn't do much for me because I was allegedly lying "unconscious" with my legs trapped between the steering column and the center console.

Conversely, my friend next to me was able to walk out of the car with the help of my friends and was rushed to the hospital with contusions and trauma.

There was, however, an unsolved mystery as to why my friends, in the other car, left me in the car while my passenger friend was taken to the hospital, unless, they left me for dead and then, only one friend stayed behind, probably to identify my body.

No other explanation can be given to their behavior and unwillingness to talk about the subject even today. Except for what I confirmed many years later as I'm about to explain.

AFTER THE WRECK:

What I'm about to tell you is the testimony from the *one* friend that offered himself to stay behind, and for whom I am eternally grateful to him for staying with me throughout all that ordeal.

Because he died years later from a terminal illness, I will discretely call him by his well-known nickname "Otto."

Those who knew him, and were witnesses to this incident, can attest to the fact that Otto stood by me from the moment my friends left the scene of the accident to the moment when my parents arrived at the hospital.

Once we reunited after my recovery, Otto told me that it took over two hours from the time of impact before I could be rescued because no one dared to touch me while I was in a convulsive state.

Note: I want you to write down the words "<u>convulsive state</u>" on a notepad, because later, I will make reference to it during our next chapter.

If you are inquisitive and sharp enough, you may have already become aware that I had claimed that I died, and may have contradicted myself by Otto's testimony. Let me explain:

During one winter day in 2014, I attended a class reunion in one of our friend's houses in Orlando, Florida.

Since I had already mentally gone through the unfolding of my transcendental experience that took place on July 7, 2011, I was ready to ask the one question I had never asked before since my car accident; and it went like this:

At the appropriate moment, I ask my friend (who was involved in the accident with me) the one question I had never asked him before:

 —*Since you were there with me, tell me the truth, did I die?*

He stared at me for a few seconds and asked me to go with him to the far end of the backyard. He didn't say a word and neither did I. I just followed him knowing that he must have something very important to tell me, and instead of answering something close to others (who might have overheard,) he wanted privacy to reveal what he had to tell me.

When he got where I suspect he felt comfortable to speak, he stopped, lit up a cigarette and with the most serious look in his eyes, he told me this:

—You were dead! You fell in my lap and I knew you were dead. I saw you—you were dead!

Puzzled by the seriousness in his tone of voice I asked,

—Then, why didn't you ever tell me?

He shook his head, took a puff and while exhaling he replied:

—How could I? At the hospital I asked for you, and everyone said you were alive! So how could I?

It took me a while to digest, but I understood his predicament. It must have taken a good three to five minutes before my other friends could pull over to the side of the road and run across over that heavily traffic area before they could reach my wrecked car.

Having a lifeless body in his lap for that long of a time would have been enough time to certify my death.

That's when I realized, I never took the time to ask, or shall I say, I was refrained from asking, until the appropriate time came.

Now, here again is where I ask you to write down another word, because in the next chapter, I will explain what the word "<u>refrained</u>" means when it comes to certain aspects you should know about, regarding these transcendental experiences.

Going back to the scene of the accident, Otto, (who along with my other friends never brought up the subject of my death after the occurrence) told me he kept waiting fruitlessly for an ambulance to take me to the nearest hospital.

Keep in mind that we are dating back to 1979 when no cell phones were available and we could only rely on the nearest public phones, or possibly someone in the neighborhood calling for an ambulance or just waiting for a police dispatch!

I had died, came back, and after going through a convulsive state, now I was a few hours away from dying from internal bleeding and there was no ambulance in sight. My life was in danger, and although

I saw what I might term as police lights, it seemed that the policeman must have kept waiting for the ambulance instead of rushing me to the hospital.

Coincidentally or by *divine intervention*, (from what I was told by Otto) a bus driver offered to take me to the hospital in his club wagon, although it was full of passengers.

And there I was, laid on the floor of a club wagon in a non-stop destination to Centro Médico, Puerto Rico's main governmental hospital, where I couldn't be turned down regardless of the severities of my injuries.

Had I been taken to the nearest regional hospital, I would've been sent to Centro Médico anyway, and not necessarily in an ambulance.

While I was being driven to the hospital, I remember feeling every bump on the road like spikes inside my guts. The pain was unbearable and in desperation, (with whatever energy I had left) I opened my eyes, saw people all around me, and there I was not knowing where I was being taken and pleading with them for the vehicle to slow down.

Strange to say, but Otto claimed that I was mumbling foul language as I pleaded for the driver to slow down.

But because I don't truly remember the words I specifically may have used, (and because I wouldn't doubt Otto's candid humor telling the story over and over again), I simply hope the driver understood my predicament and forgave my choice of words.

I couldn't say how many times I pleaded with them to slow down or how long it took for me to get to the hospital, but knowing the distance and traffic it could have been close to a full hour of driving.

But because of the nature of my culture, the driver must have broken every applicable law just to make it on time before I bled to death, and I thank him for that.

AT THE HOSPITAL:

What I'm about to give now is the chronological order of events that took place at the hospital, from what I recall and what was later explained to me from all those with whom I inquired and cross-examined following through with my inquisitive mind.

Once at the hospital, I could only be identified by name thanks to the company of Otto. I had no wallet on me by the time I got to the hospital.

If whomever took my wallet had known how valuable such a small item was regarding someone's life, no thief would have taken such a high risk in becoming a murderer by default.

I was also told that my parents were immediately notified of the accident and they both rushed to the hospital. Somehow, I must have given Otto my phone number because although I was unconscious most of the time, more times than conscious, at least I was able to reason and speak at times.

I remember how cold it felt at the hospital and asked Otto for a blanket. I remember being in the hallway next to multiple other gurneys full of people with all kinds of illnesses or traumas; not to mention the busy hallway full of noise, too much light and extreme cold.

Otto told me I kept asking for blankets and how he kept tucking the sheets under my body because I kept feeling so cold. He also told me we waited in the Emergency Room hall for hours, waiting for them to decide what to do with me. Meanwhile, I kept losing blood, therefore, I kept feeling colder by the minute.

I tried to move my legs but I couldn't. I tried touching every part of my body to make sure I was all in one piece, but only had enough strength left to drag my hands across my lower pelvic area. By process of elimination, I confirmed I had both hands and all my senses including my voice.

By the use of my hands, I found that I had a Foley catheter and that was my first sign that it wasn't just a contusion but something far more serious. Then I tried to feel my legs, but couldn't feel them.

They were both numb and that brought panic back to me. But, I was too weak to even panic and went unconscious again as the pain increased.

By the time I regained consciousness, Otto must have left because I was relocated and in a much quieter place. Next thing I knew someone lifted my covers.

The mere contact with the cold air woke me up while I heard this subtle voice asking me:

—How are you doing, son?

I was too weak to identify the source of that voice and my weakness didn't allow me to remember if I responded or not, but later, I found out it was my father who had arrived and was checking on me.

He asked me if I could lift my legs. I tried one leg but I couldn't move it. I remember trying as hard as I could while hearing the voice saying:

—Can you? Try again!

But I couldn't. It felt as if my legs were glued to the bed.

Then I heard him say:

—*Try the other leg!*

By the process of elimination, I instantly knew I had both legs on me! I couldn't find the strength to lift the other leg and now I needed to rule out if I was paralyzed from my waist down or not.

From that moment on I stopped listening to the voice command I was hearing and focused on my need to rule out paralysis. Now it was up to me!

I needed to find out by myself if I still had movement of both legs; it took all the strength I had left in me and pain was no longer a concern in my mind, now it was a matter of *Yes or No*.

In an unprecedented burst of brute force, I focused on raising my other leg and succeeded to raise it in as much as one millimeter off the gurney I was lying on. I smiled; my worst fear had been ruled out.

At least one leg was functional. As for the other leg, I had no strength left, the pain had taken hold of me and I fell unconscious again.

THE SURGERY:

Meanwhile my father was checking on me my mother kept asking for my uncle (her brother), who happened to be the head surgeon at the Centro Médico facility at the time. But to her surprise, he was out on sick leave receiving intravenous medication for an illness he was having.

Without hesitation, my mother called my uncle at his home and pleaded with him to save my life.

From what I was told, my uncle immediately rushed to the hospital to perform surgery on me against all odds.

My mother also told me that by the time he left his home, he had already called the hospital, knew how critical my condition was, and had asked for the operating room to be set up and running with a full staff so when he arrived all he had to do was scrub and immediately start surgery.

There was no argument on ethical principles for operating on a family member, nor was there a second to waste on the slim chance that I was able to make it through the surgery.

My condition was so critical that my uncle trusted no one but himself to perform such an extensive procedure, and he knew that any split-second decisions would have to be made regardless of ethical or legal issues that might have stopped any other surgeon from doing performing the surgery.

Upon his arrival to the operating room, he immediately asked to see the x-rays they had taken of my whole body. They revealed three broken ribs, as a direct result of the side impact I received.

My pelvic bone was shattered in multiple areas, but more severely from my left side and no other bones were found to be broken.

From what he could see as external injuries, I had several cuts on my face, a chipped tooth, my entire body was swollen with bruises and I was bleeding from all my cavities. Internal bleeding from the time of impact to almost 8 PM had left me with not enough blood to survive a surgical procedure and blood transfusions were administered at once.

My uncle had to perform what is called an Exploratory Abdominal surgery, or laparotomy for a better term. Not knowing what internal damage was causing the massive hemorrhage, he had to make an incision from the inferior part of my sternum to about five centimeters below my umbilicus to find the source of my internal bleeding.

Even under medication, weakened by his illness and with high fever, I was told that he performed an extensive surgery that lasted more than 5 hours.

He had to explore every inch of every organ looking to stop the hemorrhagic bleeding I was having.

By the time the surgery was done, my spleen had been removed (splenectomy) due to the severity of its damage; it was beyond repair and my uncle was forced to remove it. He also found that my left lung had collapsed due to a puncture it received when the inside of the door's decorative chrome metal trim broke in half and pierced through my rib cage and ended up piercing my left kidney. Although punctured, my kidney was still functional and left alone so it could heal by itself.

The rest of my internal organs had suffered lesions from the impact and the internal swelling had created additional internal bleeding. But there was nothing my uncle could do but to close the incision and wait. It was no longer up to him. Now, it was all up to me!

One side note I must add is that in 2012, a five-centimeter tumor was inadvertently detected on the upper quadrant of my left kidney, nearby the area where the spleen had laid, as an incidental finding while I was undergoing an abdominal CT Scan.

That proves with the upmost accuracy that when my left kidney was punctured at the time of the accident, a foreign object must have lodged there and became encapsulated over the years.

Seemingly enough, the end result must have been similar to a foreign intruder (sand) lodging inside an oyster forming and ending up as a pearl there, but in my case, ended up as a mass on my left kidney.

But because the body decays and with a slow but sure tumor growing in size and density, it had to be removed. Therefore, on December 16, 2016 (37 years later) I had to undergo a complete left Nephrectomy as a result of the kidney injury I sustained in 1979.

As an end-note to this segment, I must add that although I know that my uncle would want to remain anonymous, my heart goes out to him with eternal gratitude for saving my life! I dedicate this chapter to him and my most sincere thanks to my uncle (Tío) Ricardo.

RECOVERY IN THE ICU:

All I can remember from the surgery is opening my eyes while in the midst of the surgery and quickly being put to sleep again, more than once, I should add.

The reason being that it was unknown if I had eaten or had anything to drink, so the amount of general anesthesia was kept at a minimum, from what I was told and that was why I was kept right at the edge.

The next thing I remember was being taken to a room and having someone ask me every five minutes (or it seemed so) what was my name and address.

That became so annoying that I would just feel their presence and would recite my name and address even before being asked, just to be left alone. I just wanted to sleep. I had no concept of time, whereabouts or what had happened.

Then panic struck! And I began to shout:

—*Let me go! Untie me!*

—*Please untie me! Let me go!*

—*Not again, please, not again!*

—*I'll do anything but please untie me now!*

Suddenly, I was aware of myself being strapped by hands and feet. I remember very vividly how much fear ran through my veins, as I felt imprisoned with my hands and feet strapped.

It felt as if I was reliving those moments of torture I had endured in my one of my previous lives. I remember my inner thoughts while screaming, *not again, please, not again* and jerking each strap with all my strength, just as if I was about to break myself loose.

Then I heard someone running towards me asking me to calm down. I immediately recalled I was strapped to my hospital bed when the nurse explained to me (in between my yelling) that it was all for my safety. I immediately begged, pleaded and implored to please untie me, but then a shot in the arm knocked me unconscious.

Five minutes later, (I thought!) I was prompted to give my name, address and I still found myself strapped.

I knew by then that I was in my hospital bed and pleaded once again for my release. Again, someone approached me; I thought I was going to finally be released, and next thing I knew, a shot in my arm knocked me out again.

It felt like a nightmare that never ended: A full cycle of having to recite my name every five minutes, me screaming to be untied and receiving a shot in the arm—over and over again.

It was not until after the third day that I became fully conscious and was told that I was being held in the Intensive Care Unit with less than a fifty-percent chance of survival.

As for who asked for my name and address every five minutes, I later learned that every ICU nurse was required to ask me the same question every hour (which felt like 5 minutes to me) while monitoring my progress.

As a result, the screaming and the shot became a tug of war between the nurse and me to avoid me from accidentally removing any attachments I had from IV's to drainage tubes.

By the fourth day, I had progressed to the point of no longer requiring to be strapped or asked to recite my name. I was then released from ICU and taken to my assigned room for further recovery.

To my surprise, my roommate turned out to be my uncle Ricardo. Due to his delicate health at the time and the extensive surgical procedure he performed on me, he weakened to the extent of having to be admitted to the hospital and requested self-treatment next to me for close monitoring.

Little did I know that although I was released from the intensive care unit (ICU) facility at the hospital, I was still in serious need of medical care.

Not only was I recovering from near death, but also my body was healing from the surgical procedure performed on me.

Every tissue, from the very first incision to all my damaged internal organs, were regenerating slowly and all my system had to be at minimal function in order to be able to return to optimal condition as it healed.

And to top it off, I had contracted pneumonia from the rod that punctured my lung!

This combination was lethal and there I was still trying to make it through. Now fully conscious, I could feel the burning through my veins as I was being administered high doses of antibiotics to fight this terrible lung infection.

Having contracted pneumonia, my lungs had filled with fluid and I was in danger of drowning to death from that. The only solution was to cough vigorously in order to expectorate the fluids from my lungs.

Now the question was, *how do I do that*? I had a full twenty-centimeter suture line on my abdomen and had barely enough strength to breathe.

Fear struck when I was told that I had to cough or I would die. I'll never forget how long everyone, from my uncle to my father, attempted to convince me that I needed to expectorate. I was given every kind of advice, from the harshest to the pleading, everyone begged me to expectorate for the sake of my life.

How can you force a cough when your own mind rejects the thought of knowing how much it hurt just by the simplest attempt to breathe? I had no strength and a fresh surgical sutured area held my abdominal walls together. Just the thought as I type these lines makes me shiver with the excruciating painful memory.

I knew it had to be done, but I didn't know how *to do it.* I asked to be sedated and the answer was obviously— it can't be done!

No one knew what to do. Until my uncle came forward from the crowd, grabbed me by the shoulder, put half of his body weight on me, pressed his thumb against my larynx (Adam's apple) and as soon as he started squeezing, I began to cough vigorously.

I almost passed out, had it not been for the coughing itself which didn't allow me to pass out. I was coughing non-stop until I lost all strength and the pain in my abdominal walls was so excruciating, that finally, I did pass out.

Not only did coughing make my abdominal walls cry out in pain, but also my fractured pelvic bones felt as if I was being hammered from the inside out while my ribcage felt as if a bear hug was breaking my already fractured ribs over and over again.

What is left of my memories in my hospital bed have been put aside, and what's being written to that effect is done and over, so I don't have to recall those moments of pain again. I know what extreme pain feels like and maybe it will help others cope with pain, as I further illustrate throughout my work.

As for the accident, I never regained enough memory to give full details from my own recollection. What I know today is due to my asking others; what I was told by those friends who were at the scene of the accident; from my friend, Otto; my mother's testimony; my uncle's incidental words and my inquisitive mind which allowed me to link all the pieces together to describe what took place in perfect order and harmony to the true extent of the event.

However, as for the spiritual experience that took place, it still lives vividly within me like a birthmark I can see every day, and I can speak of it for as long as I live.

But, before I move on to my recovery, remember when I said that my survival defies all physics by body mass and weight?

Well, let me add to the equation that I've found out since, that my spleen was shattered beyond repair, or what is called having sustained a grade 5 injury.

That means that it was literally medically impossible for me to have survived over four hours of internal massive bleeding from a grade 5 splenic injury plus a kidney puncture, yet, no explanation was ever given, as to how I was able to survive it.

RECOVERY INTO A NEW LIFE:

Three months in the hospital wasn't enough time to digest what had happened to me. I was too busy recovering from the severity of my wounds and having to deal with the courtesy needed when being visited by family and friends.

Among the nurses, therapists, specialists, medication, and to top it all off, having to fight pneumonia, I had no real time to deliberate over my experience with the *other side.*

When I was finally released from the hospital to continue recovery at home, I knew my life would no longer be the same.

I remember the many times I laid in bed in my solitude while contemplating the ceiling and asking myself the following:

—Where had I been?

—Was I in a place?

—But it didn't seem like a place!

—Was it all a mirage?

—Was it all in my mind?

—Was it a product of my imagination?

—I couldn't have been unconscious, because an unconscious person simply doesn't recall! And I do recall, as clear as if it had taken place a few hours ago.

—Why was I in a dark place and not in the light?

— Was this what people call heaven?

—None of this is making sense!

—I knew I had been somewhere, but I had no physical body! I don't even recall then or now ever having a physical body!

—Why was I still myself!

—And what about those beings? Were they angels?

—What was all that swirling around me?

—And what about that higher presence; was it God?

—But it didn't look like God!

—How am I going to make sense out of all this?

—What if we all have it wrong?

—And if I ever unscramble all this, how am I going to explain it?

Believe me, there were many more questions than what I'm recalling now, but at that time my mind was cluttered by uncertainty and I might not remember in present times the multitude of questions I had at that time.

I knew something was wrong and I was determined to find out what it was. So, one day because I wanted to find out if I was being wrongly mislead by my thinking, I went to Church for advice. I still remember how nervous I was because of what I was about to do: Confess what I experienced before the Catholic priest.

I don't remember his exact words or as to what I said to the priest, but the one thing that stuck in my mind to this day is my disenchantment when I left the confessional.

I told the truth, and I was asked to say my penance for my doubting of God. I was asked to pray I don't remember how many "Hail Mary's" and an equal number of the "Our Father's," as my penance. I was so frustrated yet, I humbly complied not knowing what I had done wrong.

Due to my only frame of reference I knew I had been in the presence of what you may call God but not as it had been portrayed to me!

I knew I had been surrounded by those you may describe as angels, but I couldn't identify them as such! I knew I had been somewhere, but couldn't tell where! So, where had I been? In purgatory? And if so, what did I do wrong?

Many times I recall wondering who has it wrong: Them or me? It wasn't a dream because this was far beyond any dream. It couldn't be a hallucination or a product of my imagination because I could not have made up something that I never even knew existed.

Besides, how could I remember so vividly, with so much detail and precision, and also: How could I make up something so serious and so difficult to explain that it was already causing me so much anxiety, as it was?

After much pondering, I took a chance with my mother and asked her to hear me out. I'll never forget the usual scenario we had when conversation would take place.

My mother would stand in the kitchen on one side of the divider in the kitchen and the other person would be in the dining area facing across from her.

There were two high stools there and the other person would sit on one of them. I normally sat on the one on my right leaning over the countertop facing my mother.

I have pleasant memories of the great conversations and wisdom we shared in that particular area, also cherished by many others.

It was time for me to open myself up to my mother. Although I feared not being believed, I had to uncover every rock to find the underlying truth of my experience on the other side, so I continued. I remember being very cautious as to how I was going to initiate the question.

So I decided to play it safe and asked: *Mom, did I ever say anything during my time in the hospital about being on the other side?*

I will never forget the tone of her voice, spoken with so much loving compassion as she said:

—Oh, my son, all you kept saying over and over again was how beautiful it was over there and how you didn't want to come back.

When she said those words, I then immediately recalled someone holding my hand when I was in the hospital while I was repeatedly saying those exact words my mother had just said. So, it must have been her there with me!

That meant so much to me! From that point on, I could now attest to the fact that I indeed experienced something not of this world!

The reminiscences of the experience came to life as I heard my mother's loving response! But because I still had so many unanswered questions (that I had rather keep to myself), I bowed my head, changed the subject, and began asking questions to help reconstruct my experience at the hospital.

My mother somehow knew this was something I had to figure out by myself. I could see her predicament. How could she answer questions regarding *my* questions on Christianity when she was the one who taught me to become a Christian in the first place?

Somehow though, I knew I couldn't reach her (or anyone else) because all that surrounded me was based on those beliefs that I was questioning so much! I needed a different source.

HOW MY LIFELONG QUEST BEGAN:

I had no choice but to find the answer on my own. I was frustrated because I didn't know where to start. I couldn't talk to anyone because every time I brought up the subject, I was mocked by friends or told by the elders that it was probably a neurological reaction, due to head trauma, or a dreamlike state while I was unconscious, and the list of probables kept pouring in as I kept asking. I seemed to be going nowhere!

I trusted no one; because, no one had proven me to be righteous enough to conceive the possibility that there is something more to what we had been taught that exists.

The church teachings were out of the question. I understood my mother's predicament, my father never cared to ask, and my uncle stood by his medical beliefs and my friends were oblivious to *all* of this.

My contention was, that I knew when I was either conscious or unconscious from the clinical point of view. Meanwhile, my vivid spiritual experience occurred during the time frame between moments after the final impact and the time I opened my eyes while being rescued from my car. But no one listened.

Even my friend, who was involved in the accident, took it too lightly and I shut myself off from him as well. As I kept searching for answers I decided to keep it to myself, knowing I had no one to turn to.

My first barrier was family; followed by culture, then society, religion, science and even history, but not necessarily in that order.

Simply put, much of it, if not all of them interconnected with each other at one point or another. I had spent all my life being taught to learn the truth and here I was questioning authority!

I had no other place to turn because my world was centered on what I learned in school or what was taught to me by my religious upbringing.

Keep in mind that in 1979 all I had access to was the local library, bookstores and what you can learn from the elders. I had just graduated from High School and had not yet started college; therefore, I had nowhere to turn, I thought.

Not giving up on my search for the truth, I found myself before the one resource I had at my very own home.

It was the extensive library I had forgotten we had in our house.

My uncle had kept all his medical books stored in a room that once was my father's office. I began to look into anything and everything that had to do with the mind, randomly, because I didn't know where to start.

That's when I found writings from Sigmund Freud and Carl Young.

I was searching for that spark that could help me find the words that would resonate with what I had kept in my mind ever since my return to life after the accident.

But although both scholars' points of view were entertaining, I found nothing relevant to my experience. Then I found two books that drew my attention.

This one book was about hypnosis and the other was related to autohypnosis. None of them answered my questions but a great idea came out of them both.

How about going back to the accident through hypnosis to finally unveil the truth? *I wondered!* But I had no one to turn to; no one to trust and no one that would understand my predicament.

I needed answers, but I couldn't trust anyone except *perhaps*, *one person I knew.*

There was a psychiatrist I had visited on a few occasions for a routine evaluation. He was a referral to evaluate us as children to see if we ever were affected by some kind of marital conflicts my parents were having at the time.

None of my two sisters wanted to attend thinking they were not "crazy" but since I was the most sensible child I didn't mind and after a few sessions I kind of bonded with him.

Since at the accident I suffered head trauma, I took it as an excuse to pay him a visit and asked my father if I could go for an evaluation. My father, who kept his distance on the subject, saw it as a good idea and I immediately set up the appointment with the psychiatrist.

When I saw the psychiatrist, he was surprised to see me. He told me that once he found out I was involved in a car accident he wanted to see me, but due to the reluctance from my parents, he stop persisting.

His words gave me enough comfort to open myself up to him, but I kept myself on the fence for fear he would react like the rest of the people I had talked to.

After casual conversation and filling the gap in from the last time I saw him, I cautiously asked him, how was it I could only remember traces from the scene of the accident.

His response was that the emotional impact must have been so severe that the brain must have shut down those memories and there was no way of telling if I would ever remember them or not.

Then I persuaded him to please hypnotize me so I could go back and uncover the missing pieces from my car accident, but he emphatically refused to do so.

I tried to persuade him even to the point of giving him full authority to place his own term with regard to the process, but he still refused.

I never did tell him anything about my spiritual experience for fear of a psychological evaluation and medication, so why was he so reluctant to hypnotize me after all? I wondered!

After a few sessions of follow up visits and fruitless attempts to persuade him to hypnotize me, I gave up and cut ties with him. Today I wonder, what could have prevented him from hypnotizing me? Could *divine intervention* be the reason?

There I was, my only hope through psychology was gone, religion turned its back on me, I had no friends to turn to, my father showed no interest and my mother couldn't go against the religious beliefs she held and taught me to follow.

So I had no other option but to keep finding answers on my own, through reading books.

But how to read and trust someone I didn't even know? That's how I became a true (*)autodidact.

(*)Autodidact: One who learns from the principles of self-direction. A self-taught individual.

I stop searching for answers, and began my quest to learn how people *think* by reading whatever I could get my hands on. From psychologists to philosophers, from gurus to masters, scientists, historians, theologians, sociologists, economists, politicians, poets, musicians and the list went on, I simply needed to know how men *think!*

This was not to conform to an idea or concept but to open myself up to all the variations the human mind could expand on.

I knew what *I knew* and although I wanted to speak out, I knew my words were going to fall on deaf ears.

So, I kept on with my life, knowing that whatever I found out I was going to keep it to myself and take it to the grave. So I thought...*hear me now!*

And while I kept searching for the truth, I went to college, became a professional in the financial industry, married and fathered three beautiful children who today are young responsible adults well worth admiring.

And from the scholar to the illiterate, as well as from the humble to the extravagant, I kept learning how people <u>think</u> throughout my lifetime.

Not only did I learn how men *think*, but also, I learned from lifetime stories, family issues and personal thinking from clients, and at times I became their confident, once they knew me better. It turned out that since 1982, and at the young age of 21, I started my insurance career as a "Debit Agent."

For those who may not remember or were born after the end of the industrial life insurance era, that was a period of time when the insurance agent was given a book of active clients in an assigned territory called "Debits."

My primary job was to collect the weekly and monthly premiums from those loyal clients in order to keep them on the book, and of course, make new sales in my assigned territory.

That business structure lead to many unforgettable conversations with clients, I was visiting to collect their weekly premiums week after week. I became their financial advisor, psychologist, marriage counselor, legal advisor, and even confident for their most intimate secrets.

From Pomona to Baldwin Park, California, to later getting a transfer to Tampa, Florida, then to returning to my homeland of Puerto Rico and building a successful independent insurance agency, I met thousands of people of all races, religions, social, financial, moral, and cultural backgrounds with whom I spent many hours learning how people *think.*

I also learned much from loving people I've met throughout my lifetime. Some lifelong teachers and others, who came into my life simply as by-standers, who taught me most of what I've learned about the spirit world.

All of them, some knowingly and others unknowingly, taught me and uplifted me to where I am today by passing forward the wisdom not taught in schools.

But, I also learned to separate the deceiver from the sincere hearted and to filter the information through logic and free from theological ties. This I'll teach you throughout the ninth chapter titled *Lessons to be learned.*

That's how I became the most resourceful, stubborn, hardheaded, inquisitive, logical, and skeptical autodidact found on Earth who will not give up, until I get a logical answer that can make sense of it all.

Lessons to be learned:

§ Don't believe everything that you read.

§ There IS life after death.

§ When you cross over to the other side, you will still be you.

My message to you:

I know there's still much more to explain about in this chapter, and I do have the answers to many of those questions I might have left unanswered.

But if you would please write those questions on the same notepad (you should have next to you), I assure you that by the end of this book, I most certainly will have shed some light on many of those questions, and then some.

Keep in mind, that certain aspects are beyond the scope of this simple read, therefore, not all the answers are meant to be found in this book alone.

However, rest assured that if you hold on to those unanswered questions, I will be answering each and every single one of them, in due time, if you follow my work.

Needless to say, I sometimes look back and realize that I was only a child when I had that life changing experience. Now I know how hard it was for me to embrace the truth of the existence of a spirit world being as real as this one and yet, still so incomprehensible and oftentimes rejected by those in this plane of reality that we hardly know.

Now it is time to move on to the next chapter.

88

Chapter 4
Divine Intervention

In April 2000, my mother was dying of a malignant tumor that was originally found in her jawbone, spread through her neck and ultimately found its roots in the right hemisphere of the brain.

After aggressive radiation and chemotherapy treatments, her brain tumor kept growing and there was very little that could be done for her but to stop treatment and wait. While at home, I will never forget when my mother looked at me and in a loving tone she humbly said the following words:

— *I don't feel well, please take me to the hospital.*

Those who know me well know that under normal circumstances I'm the type of person who would question everything and I wouldn't have taken her to the hospital unless I knew it was the last resort, while still trying to figure out an alternative to the given situation.

This time it was different. Somehow, I didn't question her judgment; I looked straight into her eyes, and in an unassuming way I replied: *If you really want to go to the hospital, let's go.*

I immediately put a halt to all my business affairs and drove her to the hospital. Once we arrived, I took her to the admission's office, where they called her Oncologist; he authorized the admission and the staff started the admission process.

When my mother was given her admission bracelet, the staff left us alone for a few minutes and while waiting for the next step we both looked at each other.

I could no longer find words to keep her busy, my eyes pierced through her eyes and in the most profound moment of silence— she saw my pain.

Somehow, she could see how I was left powerless and overwhelmed, but I still showed myself to be strong although keeping it inside myself.

But my eyes betrayed me when tears flooded my eyes and the silence broke when my mother said:

—*Don't worry son; I knew this day would come.*

That did it for me. I could no longer hold my tears from showing and my silence broke as I approached her, and we hugged. She knew my pain. We both *knew* each other's pain.

At the hospital, the cancer kept spreading and within days it had spread to her windpipe.

She had to endure a (*) tracheostomy, meaning that from now on, all her communication had to be in written form.

(*) Tracheostomy is a surgical procedure to create an opening through the neck to the windpipe to ensure proper ventilation.

By that time, the Oncologist told us that there was nothing else he could do and he would have to discharge her. Subsequently, he asked for us to do the necessary arrangements to take her into a hospice facility or similar facility and the arrangements were begun.

During the evening in question, at around *9PM* and without warning, my mother suddenly went into a *convulsive state*. By convulsive state I mean her whole body went into shock and was shaking, non-stop and uncontrollably.

We didn't know what to do or how to handle the situation. Without hesitation, we rushed to call her Oncologist who happened to be making visiting calls at the hospital, and within minutes he was next to her.

He did some medical assessment and whatever else doctors do, then asked for me and my wife to meet with him outside the room.

In a somber and collected manner he told us he had just confirmed that my mother had a constricted main artery due to the tumor enlargement.

He added that he knew this was an expected outcome due to the nature of the tumor's position in relation to her circulatory system and asked us to start making the necessary funeral arrangements because she was expected to die within a few hours.

There were only three people in the room with her; my wife, my aunt, and me. As we endured the approaching solemn moment of transition, I decided to sit next to my mother, holding her right hand firmly and feeling she was acknowledging my presence even though she was convulsing continuously.

As I felt the pain of losing my mother, I silently repeated the words—*I would give up anything for this moment with you*—like a mantra, for as long as I can remember.

Those words, at that point, didn't make much sense to me from my analytical point of view, but thinking back to that day, I realize it meant that I would rather have been there with her embracing the transition of her life instead of weeping and grieving selfishly in my own sorrow.

The convulsions started at approximately *9PM*, and although it was medically expected to last only a few hours, she convulsed non-stop during two consecutive hours with no evident change.

By *11PM*, all three of us were already tired but at the same time so baffled by what we were witnessing that none of us wanted to fall asleep.

Two more hours went by and by *1AM* I still kept holding her hand with hesitation to fall asleep.

My amazement was such that I couldn't believe what was happening. *How could this be possible?* I asked myself knowing no human being could sustain such an extensive period of convulsing non-stop for four hours without the body giving up! Nor, could I understand how I was enduring sitting next to her for so long and seeing my wife and aunt not resting as well!

By *3AM*, I was still holding her hand and feeling how she randomly tightened it, making sure I was still there.

We could already see her eyelids becoming swollen and wondered how much longer would this ordeal last.

What I was witnessing was beyond reason!

By the time I looked back at my watch, one more time, it was already *5AM* and we saw no sign of relief one way or the other. We were perplexed on how the prolonged convulsions didn't subside.

Eight hours of a non-stop seizing was beyond belief. But this was real—unbelievable, but real.

But then the most astonishing thing happened when we least expected it. At the precise moment and with upmost accuracy, when the clock turned to *6AM* and the sun glimpsed over the horizon, my mother stopped convulsing, opened her eyes, grabbed her notepad, and scribbled the following words:

— I need to go to the bathroom.

All three of us looked at each other in disbelief, and after a moment of perplexity, we ran to assist with her request.

While she was in the bathroom, we couldn't believe what had just happened and began to ask each other if what we saw happening was real.

There was no logical explanation. It made no sense. What had just happened defied all possibilities with or without the medical record she had— it was just impossible!

The swelling on her eyelids dissipated with so much speed that it seemed like an illusion. What I had just witnessed for the past nine hours was something that my mind couldn't conceive, but I had to because not only did I witness what had just happened but also my wife and my aunt did as well. I had no option but to believe. Furthermore, I could attest to it with witnesses!

Once my mother came out of the bathroom, she went back to bed and took her notepad to request that my wife and my aunt leave the room, but for me to stay. We all complied— no questions asked.

Then she proceeded to write for me the following words:

—I am sorry, my son, that I doubted you. Now I know the truth. Find me a lawyer and send him to me. I have some things that need to be taken care of.

I know those writings well because I have kept all her notes in a safe place.

Although I choose not to go into personal details here (due to the legal aspects that unfolded from this transcendental experience) I will limit myself to say that when I did what I was asked to do, I learned how my mother needed to modify an inequitable handwritten will.

I complied by consummating her final requests and all arrangements were made within two months.

The sad part was seeing how my mother had to endure the painful drama that followed with those involved while resolving her legal issues in accordance to her last-minute request. Once all legal matters were settled, she died on June 7, 2000—one day prior to my 38th birthday.

Please allow me to add one more important detail to this experience that defies all physical laws: My mother died due to asphyxiation from the tracheostomy and <u>not</u> from the main artery constriction which she had been diagnosed with!

She was also found to be with full legal competency in order to make all the necessary legal arrangements, which she exercised by the full extent of the law before she died.

If you are wondering if my mother indeed experienced what is commonly known as a "near-death-experience," let me clarify that, yes, indeed it was a "near-death-experience. "

However, because I don't have her verbal or written testimony I chose to call it A Spiritual Experience.

Had my mother written in her note that she went here or there, or saw, or experienced, or someone talked with her about the experience or she had given a description of what had taken place, then it would be termed as an NDE. Can you see now why it's all a Spiritual Experience rather than limiting it to all kinds of terminologies?

As I wrote before: being a very analytical, stubborn, fact-finding person, and constantly questioning everything in order to get a logical explanation to all that surrounded me, it never occurred to me *to ask* my mother what took place during that evening in question. Let me explain:

It was a Wednesday morning around *10AM* when I received a phone call from the Nursing Home Care facility where my mother was residing while in her last days. She needed 24-hour care and to me Hospice Care wasn't adequate enough for her.

—*Francisco, come quick. Your mom is not feeling well.*

Those were the first words I heard over the phone.

—*What's wrong?* I quickly asked.

—Just come, she's really not feeling well. He discreetly replied.

I dropped everything. I didn't have time to explain my sudden exit from work and drove impatiently to see my mother.

While I was driving, I noticed that my mind was going over the entire inexplicable series of events that surrounded my mother's transcendental experience, when suddenly I felt as if I was being "disconnected" and freed up to think openly.

—She died, and I never asked what really happened at the hospital! Why didn't I ask? How could I be so blind! I reproached to myself.

I instinctively knew she had died, but I wasn't told over the phone, probably as an ethical practice among healthcare facilities. That's when I understood there was indeed *divine intervention* involved and began connecting the dots to later understand what took place.

The term "NDE" did not cross my mind, but I knew her ordeal was somehow spiritually guided.

What I know now, with the knowledge and wisdom that I have acquired throughout the years, makes it evident that my mother was taken into the etheric world and shown the adversity and injustice that would have been created had the preceding legal arrangement become fulfilled upon her death.

Likewise, she must have seen my true intent unlike what she must have been told by whom coerced her into such a wrongful legal arrangement.

That also explains why my mother asked me to forgive her for what she was misled to believe about me. Most certainty, my mother must have requested and was given an extended time to undo what would have been of great detriment to all her children.

Here is where I ask you to look on your notes and find the words "<u>convulsive state</u>" from the previous chapter.

Do you remember when I wrote that it was impossible for me to have survived my car accident? Well, if you follow the pattern here you will see how *divine intervention* repeats itself twenty-one years later.

In 1979, I died at the scene of the accident and came back by means of a convulsive state just as my mother did. But this is not the convulsive state that is medically known as a seizure.

It is a state where there is a surge of electrical activity in the brain, as the medical field would describe to explain it in physical terms.

But in spiritual terms, it is the catatonic state in which the body enters while it is being repaired by the energy source that is unknown to many of us.

Remember when I stated that I was told I was convulsing at the time of the accident, although I was previously declared dead by my friend?

And remember when I stated that all my friends, but one, left me for dead when suddenly and upon my return I entered into a convulsive state?

In essence, what took place was that my physical body was repairing itself long enough (by the energy source that is unknown to many of us), to sustain life before my soul could re-enter the body.

Twenty-one years later, my mother entered into a convulsive state for her body to repair itself long enough to sustain her life, in order for her to deal with an undertaking of something of dire importance.

As for my undertaking, mine is the work that I do, which I will explain throughout to the last chapter.

Do you remember the words of wisdom I gave you in the Note to the Reader where I wrote: *There's no mystery in life; only lack of information as to what lies ahead?*

The mystery lies in the (*) "miracle" that brought me back to life. The same miracle that reversed the main artery constraint to kept my mother alive in order for me to do her bidding:

(*) A miracle is termed as an event not explicable by natural or scientific laws.

Both mysteries (miracles) are seen here clearly solved by the words of wisdom from the Transcripts:

There's no mystery in life, only lack of information as to what lies ahead. —Transcript

Now I want you to recall again the word "refrained," as when I was refrained from asking my friend if I had died at the scene of the accident back in 1979.

In this similar situation, I was purposely refrained from asking my mother what took place during the evening in question at the hospital.

These two similar events, *convulsions* and *refraining*, are over twenty and thirty years apart, respectively, and denote in my mind one common denominator: *Divine intervention*.

One thing worth mentioning, is that my mother had a weak character when it came to decision making, especially if influenced by others.

This time my mother held so strong to her decision that I found it very unusual.

I thought her emotional strength wouldn't last long enough, but she was certain, beyond a reasonable doubt, that her decision had to be fulfilled. To me that was a *miracle* by itself!

Presently, she is doing very well on the other side. Today, we have an even closer relationship than when she was incarnated. I don't miss her at all, because I never lost her in the first place.

If you want to learn to fine tune, as well as I do, I can help you be at peace knowing that your lost loved ones are very much alive and probably doing better than when they left their physical bodies.

So far you've learned that there is life after death and that an NDE is nothing more than a spiritual experience. You also learned that you will still be you and why you shouldn't believe everything that you read.

Lessons to be learned:

§ There IS divine intervention.

§ There is no mystery in life...only lack of information as to what lies ahead.

My message to you:

Take a look back at your life and see how many times you have witnessed or have been a recipient of *divine intervention*.

Note: Although the word "divine" may be interpreted by some as coming from "God," I must clarify that because my message is being brought without theological ties, "divine intervention" does not imply divinity by deity but "divine" in the abstract essence of an influential intervention from the spirit world that cannot otherwise be described in words.

Chapter 5
How Perception Works

THIS WILL PROBABLY BE the most controversial yet most constructive chapter of all. In this chapter, I will uncover the mystery (*lack of information*) that lies in the experience one has while undergoing a near-death experience; hereby known as a spiritual experience.

One morning in 2002, I woke up like any other regular day except that I noticed my eyesight was kind of blurry, so I thought. It didn't take long before I realized that my blurry sight was not blurry but rather overwhelmed by this bright light, not hurting my eyes, but overpowering my vision.

At first, my instinct made me close my eyes and force blink them in an attempt to clear my vision, but by closing my eyes I saw no difference. The same bright light was before me either with my eyes opened or closed.

I simultaneously felt my life slowly fading away, but surprisingly enough I was tranquil and felt nothing but serenity. My analytical mind responded in an unassuming way while I realized I was heading to the same place I had been to in 1979.

This time, though, I was being "guided" by the "light" toward an anteroom to the other side.

To give you an analogy as to how the transition was taking place, imagine yourself holding two air balloons, one in each hand; one being fully inflated and the other one deflated.

Now visualize connecting both balloons by their air inlet and releasing the air from one so the air could be transferred to the other: One deflating while the other one inflates as the exchange takes place.

That's the closest analogy I can give you of what cannot be otherwise explained in words. How my physical life was fading, while my ethereal life was blooming.

It felt, metaphorically speaking, as if I was being drawn by a gentle magnetic force. There was no resistance on my part. I felt peaceful and was letting go with ease.

Somehow, I knew what was happening, not from common sense but on a deeper level. Although I didn't know what that light meant, I instinctively knew it was a passage to the other side.

While I was conscious enough, I laid my hand over my wife, who was next to me still asleep and said:

—I love you…say goodbye to the kids for me and tell them that I love them very much.

Those were the words I remember telling my wife moments before departing to the other side.

Immediately, my wife jumped out of bed and pleaded:

—YOU CANNOT DO THIS TO ME! YOU CANNOT LEAVE ME NOW!

I heard her voice distantly as if someone was shouting from a mile away. Subtly, the force that was pulling me gently subsided, allowing me to return to my physical body as if I was gently ascending to the water surface.

By the time I regained consciousness, my wife had already called 911. I heard the paramedics telling my wife that my blood pressure was very low. I was immediately taken in an ambulance to the nearest hospital as it was presumed I must have had a heart attack, so I was admitted to the hospital.

At the hospital I was given nitroglycerin pills; then, blood tests were taken, stress tests, ultrasounds, and who knows what else, were taken. Although I knew there was nothing wrong with me, every attending physician, nurse and other medical staff were telling me that I must go through all those tests to rule out whether I had experienced a heart attack or not.

But after all the tests came out with negative results; I was released with a diagnosis of "gastritis."

Although it may sound like a laughing matter, (*which ironically it is*) I later learned (through a medical practitioner friend of mine) that a diagnosis had to be given, and in this case, since all tests were negative, "Gastritis" was not objectionable, because its symptoms often times mimics a possible heart condition, so that diagnosis was the one chosen.

The incident was indeed not related to a Heart Attack or "Gastritis" as a diagnosis, but was suited better than "unknown cause."

My heart rate was surely diminishing as my physical life was coming to a close. In fact, had my wife not yelled at me, my heart rate would have come to a halt and I would have probably been declared dead due to a massive heart attack.

Can you see now how in the medical field I would have been pronounced dead? The news my wife would have received would have been something to this nature:

—*Sorry, madam, your husband died from a massive heart attack.*

While in reality, I would have simply crossed over to the other side in the most subtle and peaceful way.

Why was it that I kept having these transcendental experiences that defy all reasoning and have so much to do with experiences on the other side?

Well, keep in mind that during all those years I was totally oblivious to the true nature of those experiences by having been so attuned to the physical world.

To me, back in the year 2000, my mother's spiritual experience was a phenomenon. I simply saw it in those days as a mind-boggling event with no logical explanation; therefore, I took it as unexplainable or inconclusive with a twist of reality, as I saw the unfolding, but not really giving much thought to it, other than it was a mystery.

Likewise, the 2002 event (above) took me by surprise. And although today I can fully explain the event, (along with its true essence) back in those days I wasn't 100% certain of the validity of the experience, and kind of believed more that it was a possible physical condition that I might have had, but was never diagnosed.

It wasn't until after my 2011 experience and the Higher Truth_that was revealed to me that I began to understand the true nature of these experiences; such as, those first-hand experiences I kept bringing to the physical world to explain those "mysteries" in life.

This is the most important of all chapters, because here is where everyone gets stuck wondering how is it that many people see the light; others see tunnels, passages, heaven, or hell, and so many other perceptive ways they have learned to interpret the <u>spiritual experience</u> as they "see it."

The "light," however, is the most common of all and that one I had to experience firsthand to help you better understand how perception works. Let me explain:

Everything that you have heard so far about NDE's to spiritual experiences is the result of the *perception* that was brought to memory in order to explain what the person experienced. Let's use our imagination and not the analytical mind for now to learn this concept as a five year old would.

You should know by now that the computer language is composed of a binary code made of zeros and ones. The computer translates those zeros and ones into colored pixels, which then are transferred onto a screen monitor that can later be seen as an image by the human eye. If you ever see the binary code from a computer you wouldn't know how to start reading those codes and what makes up what those codes portray. In this particular case— an image.

Let's now use our imagination and let's make believe that the spiritual world is much like a binary code made of zeros and ones. Now imagine that those who have crossed over into the spirit world, and have come back, bring with them the memory of that experience.

How could the human brain decode the experience from the abstract world?

To answer that question, I would have to ask you to imagine the human brain having to translate those spiritual binary codes into images! How can you describe what has no words to describe? How can you depict an experience that belongs to the non-physical world?

Let's shift now. Bring back your analytical mind and look at your distant past where you have seen how the spirit world has been represented from one generation to next throughout centuries, such as visions, depictions, drawings and the like. Tell me now, isn't it true that all esoteric depictions from the past have been decoded from the abstract, by means of analogies and metaphors?

In essence, the language I'm making reference to and is coming from the spirit world as zeros and ones is nothing more than the *intent.*

The intent is communication in its simplest form, yet the hardest to understand because somehow we still don't get it!

If I could bring you to the point to understand the true value, the true meaning, the true concept, and therefore, the true definition of the word *intent*, then you would see the underlying truth in much of what is still a mystery to many of us.

The intent is nothing more than what precedes the thought. It is a bit hard to grasp when all we know comes from a thought. See if you "get it" through this way:

The <u>intent</u> proceeds the <u>thought</u>, the <u>thought</u> precedes an <u>action</u> and an <u>action</u> becomes <u>existence.</u>

Just imagine how an original intent could have become what life is today! Keep in mind that I'm not here to explain every new aspect I may bring to you! But, see it as planting the seed for when the time comes that you follow my work.

Let me help you in its simplicity with another example:

Imagine going through the hardship of going through a crossroad on your bicycle and seeing all kinds of collisions, because there's no way of knowing who's coming from the other side.

Imagine that you have the *intent* of finding a solution to the problem and start giving thought as to how to solve this problem.

Can you see how the intent precedes the thought?

You come up with an idea from a series of thoughts and begin to draw your idea from that one particular thought you liked the most. You begin to draw an octagon, give it a vivid color and write the letters "S-T-O-P" on it. Now you find a way to build it from a durable material and post it in the busiest of all intersections.

Delighted by the idea, everyone embraces the posting of a <u>STOP</u> sign at all intersections and your original *intent* becomes a creation in the physical world.

Let's read those words again, this time with a better understanding to what the intent is: *The intent proceeds the thought, the thought precedes an action and an action becomes existence.*

This might also help you to understand how creation took form. This is just another seed, for when you follow my work.

The *intent* is the first manifestation before even becoming a thought! That's how the human brain brings that spiritual intent into thought, therefore, giving it form in order to understand, depict or explain it.

When someone undergoes a spiritual experience, the intent perceived from the spirit world is then filtered through the human brain, decoded as a thought and translated into images as a means of explanation.

Since the brain is the receptor that brings to memory the experience perceived from the etheric world, the translation can only be perceived based on *preconceived* images that you can relate to.

Unfortunately, the language we once knew from the spirit world has become practically unknown to us since we have been disconnected for so long, that is from generation to generation throughout eons.

If we only knew how far removed we had become from our true nature; how disconnected we have become from our source of life; how unfamiliar we have become to the spirit world; how desensitized we have become to each other by the world we have created for our own self-gratification, and if we truly knew, then none of us would have to go through all the calamities humanity has created for themselves in this evolving world of materialistic, infinite creation, potential.

Let's now explore this concept from the beginning as someone undergoes a near-death experience (*spiritual experience*):

When the soul detaches from the physical body, as in the case of an NDE, it finds itself without a physical body in the etheric (*spiritual*) realm.

As the soul returns to the physical body, some people are able to bring back the experience to memory; and the brain, (which is a biological memory bank among other things) translates the memory into images, and then the subject puts the words to describe the experience in order to explain it.

As the intent is perceived, so is the explanation that the subjective individual gives to it!

For instance, and for you to have a clearer sense of it: if a fervent Christian undergoes an NDE (*spiritual experience*) and is approached by a spiritual being, don't expect him to describe the presence of Buddha!

Likewise, if the one experiencing feels the presence of a motherly figure and recognizes it as being what in life was his mother, then the person would attest to the fact that he saw his mother. That simple!

A great example to validate my point is one who once was known as the *sleeping prophet*, the late Edgar Cayce. He had an inherent ability to enter into a self-induced sleep state enabling him to be in contact with the unseen world.

Since his religious foundation was Christianity, the divine knowledge given to him under trance was Christian-based.

However, many insights he received from the unseen world pertained to reincarnation, among many other modalities not recognized by the Christian doctrine. In fact, for many years, Edgar Cayce was troubled by the information he received questioning its validity which was contradictory to his Christian upbringing.

But throughout the years he finally understood his purpose and accepted it, which was to leave an unprecedented legacy of "readings" the world is benefiting from today. I personally read his story and recommend you read the book, *There is a River* by Thomas Sugrue.

But why couldn't I depict those beings as Angels, if my upbringing was Catholic? Because, I was meant to bring back the experience without theological ties, this time around.

Let's go back to my 1979 spiritual experience and summarize how I described what I perceived and brought back to memory without theological ties, this time around:

I found myself in a void. I acknowledged being surrounded by other beings that filled me with peace and their love. I also felt the presence of a higher source that overpowered all my surroundings while I remained in peace. I asked myself three questions. Next thing I remember, I re-entered my physical body and I returned to the physical world.

Let me now rephrase the experience using my religious beliefs to explain the event more in tune with how many people understand things and how it could have been perceived:

I found myself in a dark place. I felt the presence of angels around me who gave me their love and comfort. I also felt the presence of the almighty God. I felt God's love and was not afraid of him. I asked God three questions, but he didn't answer. The next thing I remember was being sent back to Earth.

Notice in both Christian-base and non-theological versions how I used the word "remember."

In order to claim having an NDE (*spiritual experience*), the experience must first be brought to memory and then be translated by the brain before it can be put into words.

So yes indeed, the brain, within the neurological system, is this highly efficient receptor that by the unseen forces that bind us all, recalls the events, but not from hallucinations or neurological misfiring as science claims, but rather—It is the soul, returning from the spiritual world, with a story of magnificent proportions, eager to tell, and it's through each individual's perception that the experience is felt, lived, expressed, and as such it is told in so many ways—Transcript

I know that was a long and profound sentence but bare with me. I am simplifying these concepts as much as I can!

Perception indeed is very difficult to understand; yet its simplicity defies the human mind by throwing people off with its candor.

Let me give you an exercise I give to my live lecture audience on how perception works as a way of having the experience on your own:

Ease your mind first and clear yourself from any thought, preconceived ideas or emotions. I'm going to give you a specific word and will ask you to write down on your notepad what *first* comes to mind once you read the word I give you.

Don't over think it and once you're done, quickly put down your pen. You may write one word or a sentence as a response to what first comes to mind once you glance over the word I'm about to give. Ready?

The word is, *"Serenity."*

Each time I do this exercise in my live NDE lectures, I get all kinds of responses. Around 90% of the audience "see" water streams to woodlands, sunrises to sunsets and other beautiful scenarios as well.

If you are among the 90% of my audience, you created a thought in your brain, which translated the word into an image resembling what "serenity" *feels* like to you.

And if you are ever asked how to describe "serenity," your response would probably be: "It is like [fill in the blank]." —That's how perception works!

That explains why through an NDE (*spiritual experience*) a spiritual being's presence could be perceived as God, Buddha, Jesus, angels, and so on; and on the other hand, that explains how perception may have lead you to describe the experience as going through tunnels, pathways, doorways, the light and so many other descriptions you can relate to.

That also explains why the experience has also been described as being in places such as castles, fields, heaven, or even hell, as I've even heard people say.

As for the remaining 10% of my audience, some claim not to be able to come up with anything, while others simply change the word to *peace, love* or similar connotations.

For those, I have to ask them to describe the word they just came up with in order to explain how it felt if ever asked, and by default they must come up with an image in order to describe it. That simple!

The idea is to describe the abstract. Let me give you another quick exercise to give you more clarity just in case you fell into the 10% of my audience:

Describe the color red without using a connotation such as: *It's like...*

It's not doable. No one would know how to describe the abstract without first using a comparative method. And it's even more complicated when explained to someone that has never seen such a color.

Can you understand now how difficult it is to describe the abstract (spiritual) world?

I hope that in this chapter I have helped you understand why each and every person gives a different story to their experience with the afterlife.

Keep in mind that I'm not implying that someone that has had a spiritual experience makes up stories. To the contrary, my statement is that an etheric experience is presented to those who experience it in ways *they can understand,* can comfortably relate to, and based on the perception they are able to make a statement about for themselves and others, if ever asked.

When I say, I saw the light, I imply that I perceived what most people identify with clarity as peace, purity, the absence of matter and any other way the original *intent* was intended to be perceived by the one experiencing it.

The light was presented to me as a sign of trust, a portal, as something I could easily relate to as peace; like music to my ears, so I could let myself go without reservation

If I had moved deeper into that realm, I probably would have seen a tunnel with the purpose of helping me move even further.

Visualize it as if I had been in a dark room and someone with a searchlight was guiding my path.

I have an anecdote for the agnostic or atheists (if you will) taken from my next book *NDE, OBE and Spiritual Experiences,* that I want to share with you. I won't give too much detail because it is part of my next book, therefore, I will keep it short and precise:

A young girl, with no religious background, had a near death (or rather spiritual) experience and found herself in what appeared to her to be the woods.

She was walking through a trail and everything looked grayish to her. She had no idea where she was or where she was heading. Nevertheless, she told me during our interview that she felt at ease walking through the trail knowing she was going *somewhere.*

Her experience serves as a great example to explain how perception works and how the abstract world can be perceived for the agnostic or atheist.

On the other hand in 2013, I was taken by a spiritual entity on an (*) *astral travel*, also known as astral projection, which had I not already understood the principles portrayed in this chapter, I would have depicted the experience as traveling into other worlds when in essence I was taken inwardly into oneness.

(*) Astral travel is defined as an Out of Body Experience where the soul disconnects from the physical body and is capable of traveling into other realms.

When seen from the near-death experience oneself, *the light*, is an illusion of life itself: as it is perceived, it is believed. In 1979, I did not see the light because I had a different agenda which was to validate the existence of the void.

However, knowing the void in 1979 and having experienced the light in 2002 has helped me significantly to explain one of the most commonly known perceptive experiences—*the light.*

Let me help you understand from someone else's perspective to prove my point. Not long ago I met a man whom I instinctively knew had experienced an NDE. Without reservation, I waited for the right moment and I asked him:

—*Have you had an NDE?*

He glanced over into my eyes, shook his head to indicate he had, made a wide grin, and after a brief pause he replied,

—*I don't talk about this subject with anyone, but since you asked I will not lie to you."*

When I asked him to describe his experience, he recalled seeing *the light* and told me what he had experienced.

Seeing in him the analytical in me, I asked if he ever saw the tunnel. His answer was exactly the premise I want to bring before you as he replied,

—Frankly, I don't want to say I saw a tunnel but rather something that most resembles what you might call a tunnel. Not that I walked through it, because I came back, but…

I abruptly interrupted him with a gentle *I got it, thanks* because I knew he was struggling with words trying not to sound too crazy. That's when I told him about my work and felt his great relief from what at first he saw as an intrusion on my part.

Here is where this chapter ends as the most controversial throughout this book. If someone ever tells you of having seen under an NDE, spiritual experience, vision, or the presence of what is termed as God, angels, Jesus, Buddha, lost loved ones, or even heaven or hell, I urge you not to judge lunacy on their part because:

It is the brain (the receptor), which has brought back to memory the perception transmuted from an intent that became an image they could relate with <u>or</u> was presented to them from the etheric world as a message to give to humanity or to keep for themselves — Transcript

By now, it should be well understood that the human brain (as a receptor) needs visualization before interpretation. That is why an image must be created in order for all of us to understand there is a realm we all belong to and have forgotten due to paying too much attention to the physical world that we all have created here for ourselves.

Now, this explanation just given to you is not in conformity with the experience of those who have detached from their physical bodies (Out of Body Experiences) and have been capable of "seeing" what is taking place while outside their bodies, or hearing words across the room through walls where ears don't hear.

The answer is given throughout the next chapter in an experience termed, once again, as *divine intervention*, but from the least I expected to hear from!

Lessons to be learned:

§ The brain is the receptor.

§ The intent proceeds the thought; do not underestimate its simplicity!

§ Knowing how perception works is the key to understanding the abstract (*spiritual*) world.

My message to you:

To better help you understand how perception works, I have been privileged to have interviewed people from all walks of life who have come forward to give me their stories. Those people are the ones who have attended my live lectures and have come forward in gratitude for helping them understand what an NDE truly is.

Others have been those I have asked to interview to share their experience and gifts with the world. They all have come forward to help humanity overcome the shadow we have all been under, throughout centuries of being oblivious when it comes to understanding how the spirit world truly manifests.

From the agnostic to the devout, and to those who were mystified by the experience not knowing what to make of it, I have asked them all to share with me how they perceived the abstract in order to better help them understand what truly took place throughout their experience.

But because of the extensiveness and profoundness of its content I wanted you to read this book as an introduction to more completely understand the spirit world.

See it as having to learn to add and subtract before learning how to multiply and divide, in order for me to show you algebraic equations leading you to finally make sense of it all...*without theological ties, this time around!*

Keep in mind this book you are currently reading is equipped to help you understand, through my own firsthand experiences, the basic fundamentals of what takes place under what is commonly known as a near-death (*spiritual*). experience.

While the newest book will take you beyond the scope of my own experiences so you can enter into new dimensions as I explain each one in full detail. That will be a new journey on its own!

Note: Perception is hereby explained in the context of spiritual manifestations and how the human brain interprets such. Not to be taken as an explanation for human perception with other aspects of life.

128

Chapter 6
Out-of-Body Experiences

LATE ONE AFTERNOON, after visiting a client, I walked to my car where I had parked at the curb. As I got closer to my car I noticed a homeless man pushing a grocery cart and heading towards me. At first glimpse, he looked as if he was in his mid-sixties, dressed in rags and had a short beard.

As I kept walking towards my car I knew he was going to ask for spare change, so I swiftly reached into my pocket in an attempt to quickly brush him off with whatever change I had. To my misfortune (so I thought) I had no spare change, and since my car was parked at the curb, my distance to the car was about the same as it was from him and I knew he was going to catch up with me before I could even open the door.

I knew my only chance to brush him off was to increase my speed, get into the car, turn on the ignition and take off before he could even had a chance to say a word. But, my plan didn't work when I noticed that as I began to walk briskly, he did too.

I instinctively knew that my plan wasn't going to work and surrendered to the imminent outcome.

When I reached my car, I quickly unlocked the door as I heard the shopping cart approaching even closer by the second. By the time I was about to hit the ignition, he was already next to me. Since courtesy has always been part of my being, I lowered the window just enough to greet him, and sure enough he asked me for some spare change.

I gracefully looked down to my center console and found some spare change to give him. As I lowered my window to hand him some coins, he took them, thanked me, and waited for eye contact before saying the following words:

—*Did you know I died?* I froze. I thought to myself, why is this guy telling me this?

In that instant, a stream of calmness went through my body and my right hand let go of the ignition switch. Instead of brushing him off, I let go of any fear, apprehension, or any sense of time within me.

My analytical mind wanted to be in full control, waiting for his next move, but somehow, I knew I was there to listen and nothing else. I instinctively knew this was going to be interesting, since I was already used to having some distinctive spiritual experiences and this one looked no different from the rest.

— *Is that so?* I replied.

— *"Yes, and you know what? You go nowhere...because there is nowhere to go."*

I didn't expect that statement from him, yet I knew where he was heading. It is not that I didn't believe him, but it's just that I didn't expect such a blunt statement when all I had experienced before were manifestations from the etheric realm.

This was different; a new perspective I was not quite familiar with; a new firsthand experience I didn't see coming.

— *Is that so?* I replied again, for not having anything else to say.

— *Yes, and you can move to places... and I had lunch with a friend of mine.* He added with amusement.

— *But wait a minute...How can you move to places and eat if you are dead?* I energetically rebutted.

—*No...,* he replied with a look in his eyes that gently broke the news of what I was missing. And after a brief pause he continued.

—It is all in your mind. You think where you want to go...and boom! There you are, he said, while putting both index fingers on his forehead.

I saw in his face the enthusiasm of a child when he is about to break the news of a new realization and is about to explain how it all works.

— *"Then I wanted to see my wife and stayed by her side for a while." Then* he took a second to catch his breath and continued.

—And I spoke to her but she couldn't hear me...you know why? And without giving me a chance to reply, he continued as the child in him was expressing himself while tapping his hands against his belly and said:

—Because you need air to speak, understand? You-need air...without air you cannot be heard!

As soon as he paused, I made the noble gesture of nodding my head to acknowledge his statement. I knew I had to dwell upon his words understanding that he spoke from what he understood to be the best way to explain.

I knew he spoke from what he bought back to memory, and that his perception came from what he only knew from the physical world. That's when I felt him... and I saw myself in him back in 1979.

— *And you know why I came back?* He continued with even more enthusiasm as someone who finally had the chance to let it all out.

—*Because, you know?...I saw the doctors bringing me back to life...and I saw them all from above, working on me...and...and...I heard the nurse telling one of the doctors, 'We are losing him!'...and...and...they were saying that I wasn't going to make it....and... one doctor said, 'Let's try one more time'...and...they had this machine, you know?... that gives your heart an electric shock...and you know why I came back?*

His eyes looked straight at mine, seeking for my full and undivided attention. And in a deeper voice with much certainty, after a brief pause, he finished his sentence with upmost enthusiasm by saying,

—*Because my blood was still warm!*

Out of the whole experience of listening to him in that moment, I didn't feel as much certainty, honesty, and integrity in his voice earlier than I did from this last statement. Not that the rest of his story was less certain. It was just the degree of emotional intensity behind his last words.

I knew there was something deeper in those words. Coming from a homeless man gave me the understanding of how many of us go through a *spiritual experience* not necessarily knowing what just took place.

The word *compassion* came to me in a statement for those many having (*just like him*) no resources to know or understand through reasoning that we are not human beings experiencing life. Rather:

We are spiritual beings experiencing life through the senses — Transcript

I knew what somehow he knew, but he was unable to express well. It was just that he didn't have what was needed to fully comprehend what he knew... the very same as I knew, but couldn't understand it back in 1979.

— *And you know what?* he said, "*We are all surrounded by electricity. Everything is electricity...everything!*

That's when I broke my silence and I abruptly interrupted him asking,

—*What do you mean by electricity?*

He then extended his arms in awe and continued:

—Electricity! You know...like your cell phone, appliances, your heart and everything; everything runs on electricity. Electricity is everywhere!

Suddenly, an inner voice reminded me that his perception was accurate but perceived by his brain in ways only he knew—electricity! In essence, what he meant was that everything around us is <u>vibration</u>! From the subtlest vibrating, to the one vibrating force that creates all that is and exists.

I wasn't about to confront him with a game of words, as many of us do from time to time. I just knew exactly what he meant and nodded my head acknowledging his words.

At that point, I realized he had run out of words and knew it was my time to validate him. So, I took upon myself the role of cross-examining him.

—So, tell me, how did you die? I asked, in an unassuming way.

—Because I got hit by a truck, he replied, while his body language and tone of voice lead me to believe his words.

—And wasn't that truck driver supposed to have insurance? I asked.

— *"Yes, and my lawyer is fighting for a settlement right now.*

Little did he know that he gave me the perfect opportunity for me to keep questioning his credibility. Being retired after thirty years from the insurance industry gave me an excellent opportunity to test his integrity.

So I discreetly proceeded with my interrogation process, just as if I was eager to learn more from him and not to blow my cover.

To my surprise, this homeless man answered every question and provided me with accurate answers to the insurance claim process along with all the contingencies one has to go through while pursuing an insurance claim with utmost accuracy.

His integrity ratified two things; he was telling me the truth, and he was not crazy.

Once I ran out of questions, I patiently listened to his extensive answers before taking this conversation to a close.

With utmost politeness, I told him I needed to go and I wished him the best of luck with his insurance claim.

Because I couldn't blow my cover, I refrained myself from giving him any advice with his insurance claim (as I normally would) but, somehow, I felt at ease knowing my place was to listen and not to intervene in his path.

I took my eyes away from him and when I was about to turn on the ignition I heard his voice once again.

—*Wait!* He abruptly interrupted me.

—*Let me show you.*

He raised his shirt and exposed his abdomen to me to show me the last piece of evidence to attest to his validity. What I saw left me perplexed while shivers ran down my spine.

I saw before my very own eyes this man's surgical scar having an almost identical length, width, and scar line around the navel as mine. I did not want to blink my eyes for fear I was imagining things.

Not a word was exchanged and he let me go not without first giving me a solemn final message.

As I headed back home I remembered this homeless man's last words repeating in my head and picturing the look on his face when he got even closer to me, leaned over the driver's door and into the window and before letting me go, he said the following words:

—I'll let you go now, but we will meet again, because I have more things to tell you.

As I drove away, I kept looking back into my rear-view mirror to confirm that this man was real and that I wasn't hallucinating.

Why would I meet with this man again? What else would he have to tell me? I kept pondering restlessly.

I still had a full day ahead of me. I had much work to do, but interestingly enough I lost total interest in continuing work this day and instead I headed back home.

I must have driven on automatic pilot all the way through, because I don't remember how I got home but I do remember going over this experience that was stuck and repeated in my mind over and over again from the moment I saw the homeless man to the moment I reached home.

I had to figure out what had just happened. I had to confirm that what took place was for real. I had to decipher what he meant by his last words, and most importantly— who was this guy?

The next day I made up my mind to see him again to get straight answers to stop theorizing and to ease my mind.

I drove to the same location, at approximately the same time frame that I saw him last. I drove around block after block looking for him. I knew the homeless keep themselves within a close radius because they have no mode of transportation other than their own feet and a shopping cart. But this character was nowhere to be found.

Then an inner voice gently reassured me that I would see him again, but not as a homeless person next time around. Needless to say, I did met him again a few years later, in an amazingly true story which I will tell as soon as I finish explaining what this homeless experience led me to understand.

Following this incident, I began to reflect on the whole experience and saw with clarity what in essence took place. I was being given the answer to what is commonly termed as an OBE (Out-Of-Body Experience.)

I began to see clearly that an OBE takes place when the physical body is left behind and the soul keeps enough consciousness to stay within the boundaries of the physical world.

What the homeless man taught me was that many of us don't understand what takes place within an OBE and conclude that once you die you go "nowhere."

For those who believe that one should be going through a tunnel of light, or be taken to heaven, or that they will find themselves surrounded by loved ones who have passed over, <u>*but* instead</u>, find themselves (while transitioning) hovering over and above themselves, with enough consciousness still linked to the physical world, may feel cheated, dismayed, or may end up believing that it was all a lie and that there is nowhere to go.

Those may also be the many souls ending up hovering around and above themselves, commonly known as "lost souls," not knowing there is_Higher Truth they must seek beyond the veil they have created for themselves. Sound familiar?

You can see it every day as it takes place in our daily lives: People who see only the negative side of life, the depressed, the obsessed, the alcoholic, the drug addict, and the mentally ill, just to name a few.

They are people who have created their own world limited to their beliefs, and it isn't until someone gives them a helping hand that they are able to see the bigger picture beyond *their* reality. Sound familiar, also?

I am here to help you see the bigger picture; the one I could see from a distance, beyond imagination, so you can awaken to the true reality of our existence, for I have seen it, lived it, and experienced it myself, bringing it back into memory to help you remember where you came from and to find what I like to call the way back home.

The fact that the homeless man couldn't speak with whomever he wanted ratified that he was in the etheric world with enough consciousness to see his physical surroundings.

His understanding that air was needed for his voice to be heard further confirms that he was in a realm that couldn't manifest what he intended for lack of support, i.e., matter does not exist in the non-physical world, hence, no molecule can be moved to create a vibrating sound as an etheric soul attempts to emulate words.

NOTE: Let me clarify that "spirits" <u>do</u> communicate with the "living" by their ability to vibrate at a level that can only be extensively explained separately, but for now, let's keep it simple at the level purposed in this book.

As I pondered about it, I understood why he became so emotional and expressive when he said, "...because you need air to speak."

Imagine the frustration that he must have felt while attempting to communicate through sound or movement fruitlessly while in a new environment where he found himself so unfamiliar with!

Great examples of what I'm conveying, are portrayed in films such as *The Other's, The Sixth Sense,* and *Ghost*, just to name a few.

But keep in mind that I'm only making reference to this specific subject as examples, and not necessarily to certain fictional theatrical precepts implied in the above-mentioned films.

But how was he able to see with his eyes closed and even listen to the operating room staff while Out of Body? Simply put—through the *intent*. It's not through the physical body and its senses, that the one experiencing captures the *experience* when Out of Body.

While in the body, life is perceived through the senses: Receptors that pick up the vibrational forces of creation and the brain translates each experience through the five senses which are sight, taste, smell, touch, and sound.

But when you are Out of Body, it is you as a soul who picks up the *intent*. See it as telepathy, needing no explanation because the intent is all that's needed. See now why I said not to underestimate its simplicity?

However, when a person re-embodies, like in the instance of a death or near-death experience (*spiritual experiences*), what we bring to memory from the spiritual realm (*not from hovering over the physical plane, I must clarify*), is the intent from the abstract (*non-physical*) which must be first filtered through the brain, give it form, and ultimately understand through perception. Can you now see the difference?

Since I know this may not be so easy to understand, let me explain it in a different way:

When someone has an Out of Body experience and the soul keeps enough consciousness to stay within the confinements of the physical world, the intent from those in the physical plane is perceived by the soul and the vibrating forces from those around the one having the experience is picked up as well.

That's why the one experiencing recalls words and actions that take place within their immediate surroundings, and can even travel distances, like the homeless man said about visiting his wife and friend.

However, when the soul detaches from the physical body and moves into the spiritual realm, whatever is brought back to memory, must be first filtered through the brain in order for the abstract to be explained by the one experiencing it as it was perceived.

In both instances, the *intent* is the driving force and perception is the carrier.

Let's take *hearing* for instance. Let's say that while you undergo surgery, your loved ones are having a conversation in the hall.

While your soul is in the operating room you won't hear a word they say. But, the instant you detach from your physical body and focus your attention on the whereabouts of your loved ones, you pick up the vibrational force of the intent that surrounds them.

Soon you become aware of their presence and focus even more on the intent of one or the other while they are having a conversation. Quickly then, you pick up the vibrational force that emanates from both and interpret either verbatim or with similar connotations of what is being said.

If the impression is strong enough for you to bring to memory the moment you wake up, you may even be able to repeat their exact words when asked.

Now, let's take *eyesight*. Say for instance, that the surgeon sees your blood pressure dropping. Once you detach from the body, you as a soul pick up what is taking place and pay close attention to what the surgeon sees.

Not to be confused by a direct visual interpretation, but rather, what the vibrational movement of the blood pressure gauge means to the receptive mind (*the surgeon*).

As you perceive the intent before the action, the visual image is perceived and "picked up" by you and then translates it to what you "saw."

Another great example that I can give you is in the Transcripts that I receive, perceive and transcribe from the *Collective Forces of Knowledge and Wisdom*. I first receive them in abstract form as what you may term as a concept. I perceive what the original intent wants to convey.

Then depending on the relevance of the intent, I may perceive an image that serves as a guide for me to follow while the thought process begins to take form. Please allow me to further elaborate in chapter 10 to follow up.

On occasion, I perceive the intent as an indescribable feeling, that I must find the words to convey. If I err in my interpretation, the intent is rectified by repeating itself through a stronger or weaker feeling making me retract from that specific word or concept before moving forward.

In other instances, it simply becomes a drawing or visualization as I advance from an intent to a thought and then into images following a recognizable pattern, which then becomes a portrait serving as a metaphor or analogy which I can put into words.

One great example, is the front cover of this book. The blackboard and drawing image was the result that came about after I asked the *Collective Forces of Knowledge and Wisdom* to help me explain in simple terms what a near death experience truly is.

Amazingly enough, the image was drawn by me as I kept visualizing the abstract and while drawing lines as I interpreted the intent.

As for the language (English or Spanish), it is of my choosing, although I sometimes feel drawn to write in Spanish depending on the source's inclination. If I had been able to speak Mandarin, by all means, I could choose to write in that language too. In other words, I choose how to deliver the message by using the appropriate words that best fit the original intent.

The reason why I use English (although is not my native language) is in part because I was unknowingly lead to move to Florida to begin my work in this language. Maybe it's because here is where I'm supposed to start— only source knows!

I know all this may be kind of mind blowing to you, but let me make one more attempt to help you "see" it with more clarity because *I really want you to get it.*

How can you see things in a dream with so much detail while your eyes are closed?

How can you smell, run, laugh, cry, hear, speak, see and so on while you are totally asleep?

If you arbitrarily decry that this example is not applicable as being real, let me clarify that although you may think otherwise, in reality, the physical plane is an *illusion*, and the soul keeps experiencing life while the body rests—another seed planted for you to work with!

Moving forward with Out of Body Experiences, let me clarify that not all who have had an OBE simply stay in physical consciousness and come back. There are many others who go through an OBE before moving to the next level (aka, *"The light."*)

Let me give you one particular experience I learned from someone experiencing an OBE while I was leading one of my NDE support groups some time ago.

This lady was in her seventies, and was troubled because while in her thirties she experienced an OBE while undergoing surgery for a life-threatening ailment. Her consternation was not that she had an OBE, but rather, that while having the OBE she suddenly saw what she referred to as a bright light in a tunnel and felt like it was pulling her toward it.

Her contention was that even though she felt attracted to the light and in peace, she was deeply concerned for her children. She was not fond of the idea of leaving her children behind.

She also remembered being asked, through an inner voice, if she really wanted to return even though her body would have to undergo a prolonged and painful recovery, to which she agreed and returned to her physical body.

She told me that after the surgery, the recovery period was extensive and very painful, but she chose to return for the love of her children, and she did not regret it at all.

What troubled her the most, after the experience, and the reason for her sharing the story with me, was that she had wondered all her life how was it that she experienced both, an OBE and the light in the same incident. My response to her applies to anyone with a similar experience:

When the physical body gives up, and if there are strong attachments to the physical world—as for instance, love for those you're leaving behind, confusion, fear of the unknown, unfinished businesses or similar attributes—the soul, preceding the physical body, would rather keep holding on to what it knows best, and if given the choice, it would choose to stay.

I'm not saying that when the time comes, you had better move on or else you'll end up trapped in the limbo, or purgatory. It is *you*, the disembodied soul who chooses what's best for you when the time comes, unless there are other chartered plans for you!

In her particular case, the children were what attached her to this physical plane. When her body was about to give in, she was given a choice to move on in one direction or the other by means of a choice between a new realm (*through the light*) or back to the physical plane.

Had she stayed in the OBE state a bit longer, there probably wouldn't be a strong enough catalyst to return to the physical plane she had to choose, and fast.

Another great example of the latter, was an incident that took place in my hometown back in 1975 with a local media celebrity.

One particular day, she was at the beach and chose to dive into the water one last time before heading home.

Unaware that the tide had subsided, her head hit the sand and broke her spinal vertebrae.

The broken spine left her confined to a wheelchair for life, and this is what she had to say:

She revealed in an interview that the moment she suffered the incident she immediately saw her physical body (OBE) floating in the water, but felt no pain.

She noticed that water, salt, sand, and algae were molecules separated one from the other, like the essence of everything that is and exists in the physical world (*what we know as matter.)*

She recalled peace abounding in her while not in the physical body. Beside her, (*herself as a soul)* there was also a greater presence she reluctantly wanted to describe by name, but I understood she meant "God," since I experienced the same reluctance throughout the years for the connotation given by multiple religious beliefs.

She recalls being given the choice not to return to her physical body if she didn't want to, and if she did, life would be hard.

But after being taken before the presence of her living father and after seeing the affliction that her death would bring to him (*attachment*) she chose to return to her physical body.

Upon her return to her physical body, she recalls herself drowning, unable to move her extremities and seconds later, she was rescued.

Her recovery was extensive and challenging; nevertheless, she came out with an amazingly positive attitude, continued her active role in the children's' entertainment business, and today she is a living example to many.

Notice the details throughout this OBE experience:

(1) She did not recall seeing the light, a tunnel, or any similar experience. But rather, she found herself and her surroundings as particles of matter; like consciousness of the basic elements in the physical world, while she was in spirit form.

(2) She perceived the presence of a Higher Power she was reluctant to describe.

(3) She recalls being given a choice not to or to return knowing life was going to be a hardship.

(4) She was taken in spirit to see her living father.

(5) She chose to return due to attachments, in this particular case— to her living father.

Lesson to be learned:

§ An OBE is a spiritual experience when there is enough consciousness to keep the soul connected to the physical world.

§ An OBE can be stationary or the soul can travel distances.

§ I've known many who claim to have the ability to go *out of body* at will.

My message to you:

When it comes to spiritual experiences, each experience is as individual as there are souls. There will be many manifestations in common; but also, each individuality trait brings with it experiences that will defy any preconceived idea of how it should be manifested. That's why I'm so reluctant to use any other word or connotation, other than a *spiritual experience*!

Perception plays a significant role in deciphering what the experience meant rather than what the experience was. As unimaginable as it may seem, it is equally true for someone to claim having seen the atomic particles of the elements under an OBE as it is for someone else to claim seeing a God figure through a spiritual experience. It is not what has been *seen* but how the brain interprets what is brought back to memory from the etheric world.

Remember: You are the sum total of your experiences since the first movement took form—Transcript

Since you are the sum of all your experiences since the first movement took form, it only makes sense that *perception is as individual* as there are souls!

Chapter 7
Making Sense Of It All

Remember the homeless man who told me we were going to meet some other time because he had more to say?

Well, about a year following that experience I drove to South Florida with my wife on business trip. We stayed overnight at a hotel near a cosmopolitan area that my wife wanted to explore and also dine there during evening hours.

Because I was not familiar with the surrounding area, we chose to take the hotel shuttle to drive us around and help us choose a good dining place. When the shuttle arrived, the driver happened to be a young dark-skinned fellow (with a friendly personality and very talkative) greeted us in a very enthusiastic fashion and drove us to our destination.

Compelled by his friendliness, my wife and I started a conversation with him and learned that he came from the Caribbean Islands and made it to this country in search of a better life for him and his children. His spoken words were somehow profound and very articulate.

My wife, who happens to be a passionate positive thinker, began asking questions regarding how happy and positive he seemed to be.

Little did we know, we had unleashed the motivational speaker in him! It didn't take long before I realized we were driving around the same road twice and we were about to drive in the same area one more time; but, I remained patient because his speech was very eloquent.

Then, I interrupted and asked him to pull over so he could continue the conversation without driving around.

When he finally pulled over, I asked him about his educational background. He replied that he had no college degree and other than his state of mind which was knowing that this life is not what we all had been taught it to be.

He told us that since he was a child, he always had known more than what many scholars claimed to know, but because of his lack of education, all he could do was to live life knowing what *he* knew.

Suddenly, while in the driver's seat, he turned his head and shoulders towards me, made eye contact, and I saw the look of the *homeless man* in him. I froze and the next set of words sent shivers down my spine:

—*There are many like me, knowing more than what other people know, but have no one to turn to and we keep it to ourselves. We are many out there that can be reached...many!*

I smiled at him, became teary-eyed and acknowledged his words. That was the end of the conversation because after that he proceeded to drive us to our destination and the rest of the conversation became distinctively mundane.

While he was driving, I told him I was an author and gave him my business card, which he took with gratitude.

One detail I must add before I end the story is that when he pulled over to drop us both off, and before I opened the door to exit the van, he turned around. and asked,

—*Sir*, he politely said, but showing confidence as to what he was about to ask me. Then he said, *I appreciate you giving me your business card, but why should I keep this business card?*

Because I never would have expected such a profound question from anyone, I was perplexed and taken by surprise as I never would have thought I would reply as I did when I said:

—I don't know! Maybe next time you hear from me, I could be giving a symposium and if you keep that business card, and show it to me and I recognize you, I may take you with me!

He nodded his head and we both smiled at each other as if saying, "touché." The next day, I looked around to see if I could see him again, just to take a last impression before departing back home.

I was not much surprised that I could not find him but gave little thought to it because, let's just say I already knew.

To this day, my wife is still confused and in disbelief about what took place, and it has taken me a while and much patience to make her understand what many may consider as a product of one's imagination.

Others might think that what took place, in both instances, were angels or spirits appearing and disappearing throughout the experience.

Although I might feel the impulse to let myself be drawn to the belief that they both were "angels" that crossed my path to deliver a message, I would rather keep the experience at a level in conformity with my mission: To deliver the message without theological ties, this time around. Let me explain:

The homeless man is probably still homeless. It is not that the homeless man was a ghost that suddenly appeared out of nowhere just to relay a message and then disappeared into the ether. He was probably one of many who have had an "Out of Body Experience" and is still unaware of what in essence took place, and in his case, may still believe that we are surrounded by electricity.

And perhaps also, neither did the driver became an usher to relay a message and then vanish from Earth. He was indeed one of many who know more than many scholars do, but had no one to share his knowledge with.

What took place was that, as there is *divine intervention*, these types of manifestations are among many I have experienced, and I have had the good fortune to acknowledge first hand (and with a complete understanding) of what had taken place.

The homeless man was an ordinary person who had an Out of Body Experience. But, because he was probably susceptible to divine intervention, a spirit of light was able to manifest through him to help me better understand what an OBE is, and then he moved on.

And at the same time, the driver's state of mind presented itself as a great opportunity for the same spirit of light to manifest itself while this young fellow's emotions were at its peak, relaying a message only I could understand.

I'm most certain both individuals would remember the event and probably what they said. But also, they both would most likely look at me as if I was kind of delusional if I were to explain to them what I'm explaining to you at this time. Now, as for how do I know that they both became instruments of the same "spirit of light" delivering a message? Here is how:

I was able to see in both individuals the same look, the same emotion, the same feeling, and the same intent that only I could understand that was being manifested through them! Especially that same penetrating look they both gave me as if coming from the same *source*.

Let me ask you:

Have you ever spoken to someone and suddenly words came out of you that you have no idea where they came from?

Have you ever been in a place and suddenly you have a unique urge to help someone only to later find out that your actions were not your usual behavior?

Have you ever been compelled to call for someone's attention to later find out you saved him or her from a fatality?

That is *divine intervention*. One that happens every day and at all times.

Let me tell you an anecdotal situation that I experienced not long ago. While visiting an old friend, and enjoying his company for hours while exchanging topics of all sort.

I knew him well enough to know that close to 50% of what he was saying was either an overstatement or half-truth. But since we were old buddies, I knew this and allowed it to pass as I normally did for the sake of friendship.

When the day was over and we were calling it a night, I said some words I would never have thought I would say to him. Those words I choose to keep to myself, because if he reads this book he would know I'm talking about him. They were very specific in content and the look on his face told me he was baffled hearing those words from my lips.

To this day, I know I became the vehicle by which those words were revealed to him. Needless to say, more and more often, I have become the instrument by which people receive messages from words I've said, and not necessarily knowing myself why I said them, either by anecdotes, phrases, statements or simple words.

These events, and many others, are examples of spiritual intervention only manifested in those who are attuned, receptive or simply opened to perceive. The messengers may never realize the magnitude or repercussions of their words, or might never realize that they became the instrument by which, *divine intervention,* took place.

For the rest of humanity, it would simply be seen as chance, coincidence, or simply awkwardness on their part.

The fact that in both instances I wasn't able to go back and see the homeless man or the shuttle driver again is also indicative of spiritual intervention.

This pattern has been accounted for over and over again by many throughout their lifetime, and most are unaware of what had taken place.

Keep in mind that if I had found that person the next day, and if he didn't clearly recall what took place or if he remembers it at a very superficial level, then I would probably talk myself out of it in disbelief. Make sense?

It is not the flesh that needs to be recognized but the spirit that transcended in the individual who delivers the message. —Transcript

However, if I go deeper into the subject, from what I have been told, many are those who have claimed to have seen a person who delivers a message and in the blink of an eye that person disappears. Those are the ones who can even describe them, and then are told that such a person does not exist. Let me give you another case from the forthcoming book *NDE, OBE and Spiritual Experiences* to help me better explain:

In one of the interviews I conducted while writing that book, this particular person told me that, while in the maternity ward, she claimed that a male nurse kept waking her up to remind her that everything was going to be ok.

After giving birth, she wanted to thank the male nurse and asked for him to come over to thank him. To her surprise, she was told that there was no male nurse at the maternity ward. During the interview, she later told me she found out it was an *angel* giving her strength.

After I heard her story, and along with my new awareness from my two incidents (the homeless man and the shuttle driver), and after both having the same ending; the sudden "vanishing" of the person, I wondered if my experiences were also divine intervention through an apparition, opposed to divine intervention through (*) trans-mediumship.

In other words, what I previously explained as spirits taking spontaneous control to speak through you, and leaving without you even noticing.

(*) Trans-mediumship: The ability to go into a trance and allow spirits to speak through them.

As you can see, this subject is extensive, therefore I suggest you read the forthcoming book *NDE, OBE and Spiritual Experiences* to learn more in depth all about the spirit world. Not only from my own first hand experiences, but also from those I personally interviewed on a one on one basis while making direct eye contact.

Those are a few out of the many who have also taken a glimpse at the other side and attest to the veracity of that other world; not to mention, a bonus chapter interviewing respected psychics and mediums to help me better explain to you what lies ahead.

Now let's move on and fuse all those experiences into one so you can make sense of it all.

A spiritual experience can range from visions, dreams, apparitions, mystical experiences, manifestations, Spiritually Transformative Experiences (STE's), Near-Death Experiences (NDE's), Shared Near-Death Experiences (SDE's), Near-Death-Like Experiences (NDLE's), Out-of-Body Experiences (OBE's), Exceptional Human Experiences (EHE's), Nearing-Death Awareness (NDA's), After-Death Communications (ADC's), and many other terms that humanity has come up with to describe what I convey in total as a Spiritual Experience.

Likewise, spirit communication like Clairvoyance (seeing), Clairaudience (hearing), Claircognizance (knowing) and Clairsentience (feeling) among others are nothing more than modalities by which there is communication with the spirit world.

Divine intervention has been proven many, many times, through eons, but when science is involved (although it cannot be disproved), it's never acknowledged due to its inability to be scientifically replicated. Of course not! Because the spirit world does not belong to the physical world!

Science cannot yet acknowledge a spiritual experience, because it cannot be measured by any scientific method known to man.

Ironically, science has proven itself through history too often to be wrong, reshaping one theory after another, and somehow it's often taken as true, only later to be found otherwise.

Meanwhile, spirituality has been consistent in its statements: that we are spirit in nature; there is life after death; there is a spiritual law of Cause and Effect; that divinity exists; the Golden Rule; the precept that holds the vibrational force as valid, and knowing there <u>is</u> a source of life, which has been given many names, but is only One.

Since this chapter is all about making sense out of all of this, let me help you expand your mind and introduce you to another realm you experience every day but are unaware of —it is your *dreams*!

Have you ever recalled a dream so vividly that you remember the experiences such as having laughed, cried, ran, sweated, became tired, seduced, deceived, angry, compassionate and many other experiences, as if you had lived them in the flesh?

What people dismiss as fantasy is actually an experience you had, as the soul you are, while the body rested. Nevertheless, it is an experience you will carry with you for the rest of your existence.

What people don't realize is that while in their dream state many conflicts get resolved, (as part of our existence), on our journey, while the body rests.

The mind is you and you are the mind. It is so simple, yet, in its simplicity is where humanity gets stuck by looking for other ways to explain what has already been explained before, with all kinds of analogies, multiple metaphors, different words and we still don't get it:

You are the sum total of all your experiences since the first movement took form. —Transcript

You may be here in the flesh or you may be here in spirit form; you are still going to be YOU. Your mind is you and you are your mind. And your essence comes from the abstract, the realm where the soul manifests in spirit form, which precedes the body and other forms as well. That's another subject worthwhile expounding on in some other writings.

When you sleep, your experiences are lived within you, because you ARE the mind. When you are awake, your experiences are lived by you, and what you collect and recall to your memory, is of the mind and not the brain.

The brain is simply the receptor, or the translator, if you will. And when you die, your soul, which is YOU, will no longer have contact with the physical plane of reality; nevertheless, it will move on to new realms, to experience life in other forms.

As for those who can communicate with them *(spirits)*, it is because one must be able to vibrate at a frequency level compatible with them in order to communicate through those available modalities as know from yesterday and today.

After passing on, some people have learned to fully detach from the physical plane and move on to new realms, while others, due to attachments, choose to vibrate at lower frequencies in order to mingle in the physical realm, *or stick around if you will.*

I strongly urge you to learn more of the spirit world by reading my next book, NDE, OBE and Spiritual Experiences.

Lessons to be learned:

§ Divine intervention happens more often than you may think.

§ A spiritual experience is a glimpse into the other realm of existence that coexists with us.

§ When you are asleep, awake or disembodied, you are still going to be YOU.

My message to you:

Being spiritual is experiencing life independently of any specific religious context, knowing there is one God or Higher Power, one purpose, one truth, and it must be found within you.

As for God—that is life in its purest form and the one force that binds us all together. And the force is <u>love</u>, which gives us peace, and by giving love one reciprocally receives peace, and thus love gives you peace.

As for our purpose—it is to return home. That place you call home is where you go to rest: a safe place, where you seek refuge, where you seek peace, where you seek love, where you seek comfort— a place to rest. And home is not a place to dwell, but is within you. It is where you can discover that you are <u>one</u> with Him, ONE within, the individuality of the self, but knowing deep inside that if you merge, all pain will go away and all the desiring will go away—for the wishing will stop needing, and the soul will stop wanting. And you merge in divine consciousness of what creation is, and are no longer in need to find true peace.

And as for truth—It is the one that must be found within you. —Transcript

170

Chapter 8
Let's Get Legal

REMEMBER THE THIRD CHAPTER, where I wrote *Peace was all I felt, (and so will you,) for as long as you do the right things in life?* Well, here is where I explain that as promised:

By now, we all know that an NDE, OBE, or spiritual experience is a glimpse at the other side. Once we return from the experience, we may recall what has been kept in memory, make sense of it, renew our lives, and seek for Higher Truth. But, what if we choose not to return? Or, our physical body perishes and you can't come back? Or, we are told our time is up?

It is easy when one comes back and has time to reflect, make amends, and straighten out what needs to be put in order for when the time does come—but again, what if coming back doesn't take place even if you want it to?

What took me over thirty-five years to learn from my Death Experience, to seeing the light, and from the Transcripts (which are concurrent with ancient writings), is that we, (when the time comes, whether we are ready or not)— we *have to go.*

One thing is having a death, near-death, out of body or spiritual experience and coming back by choice or decree and another is having the experience and not coming back. Who are we leaving behind? How much unfinished business is left undone?

That brings me to the one subject I have not seen being mentioned when it comes to spiritual experiences, that is the realization that we may be leaving someone behind along with some unfinished business that someone will have to resolve after our departure. Not to mention those unfinished businesses *of the soul.*

One of the most commonly-feared instances holding people back from letting go when the time comes, is the uncertainty of how their loved ones will handle life in their absence; from the emotional and financial issues and from the simplest to the most complex of legal matters.

Take, for instance, my year 2000 experience. Had my mother died without properly resolving her legal issues, we would have found ourselves in a legal battle of immeasurable proportions.

Likewise, had I gone through the light in 2002 without providing adequate financial support, my wife and kids would have ended up in financial hardship.

Unfortunately, many people still believe in the old myth i.e., *It won't happen to me*. Trust me, I know this subject very well because I have had to deal with it throughout my entire business career.

Having helped thousands of people with their financial and legal issues, after a loved one dies, has helped me to see what is "on the other side," not from the spiritual point of view, but from the legal and financial aspects that the surviving spouse has to go through.

Trust my words! If you think that by simply "letting go" and living an oblivious spiritual life will set you free when you move on to the other side, you are in for a big surprise.

After reading *this book*, ignorance will no longer serve you well because now you have been informed as to what is to be done before you depart and what it takes to be at peace with yourself and others.

Trust me on this one, too: There is no harder experience for those who know their life is coming to a close and seeing their legal and financial issues being unresolved and not being able to do anything about it. In many cases, I have witnessed where the critically ill have asked me what else could be done to undo the inadequacy created by ignorance or negligence on their part.

Let's start with you in the first place. Remember the golden rule? *No harm should be done to yourself or others*—better known as: *Do not do unto others that which you do not want done unto you?*

Let's then toy with it for a moment. Let us say, for instance, *(and to prevent the event from happening)* it happened yesterday. You kept on living life thinking that when the time comes you won't give it a fight and will move on to a better place.

Let's also say that you became critically ill and had to be rushed to the hospital. Now let's say by the time you arrived you were admitted while unconscious and you went into a coma.

Let's further elaborate that you were clinically declared to be in a vegetative state and within hours, all but one of your children proposed to keep you on artificial life support.

But before I continue with the story, I must make a disclaimer to the fact that I am not a lawyer and none of what is written throughout this chapter constitutes legal or financial advice. These are only scenarios I am portraying and not actual events. Any similarity with this and any other events is purely coincidental— Francisco Valentin.

Let's explore further, and say that a legal battle unfolded when that only child (who knew you) wanted you to move to a better life and is now forced to fight a legal battle, because you never signed the most important document that would have saved your soul from this event— that is a *living will* establishing your desire not to be kept on artificial life support.

In its absence, a petition was filed and the county judge ordered your feeding tube to be kept against your son's will. The battle continued, and after years of legal contingencies, your estate is depleted, family quarrels have broken them apart, and you count every second that goes by like an eternal condemnation for the wrongdoing you have done to others and yourself.

Let me warn you that having the soul detached from the body makes no difference, because it is still you who sees yourself bound to the pain you are causing to others and are unable to go forward *(into the light)* until that battle is resolved.

It is like being on trial and not being able to walk away from the testimonies and complaints you could have avoided with the simple power of a pen, for as long as the law and your estate would allow.

Ask yourself if you want to be part of that scenario while we toy with another scene you may be interested to be part of:

During one particular evening (*I will use past tense, to prevent the event from happening*) you went to bed like any other day, taking life for granted and not knowing that when each one of us goes to sleep, the soul may decide not to come back, either by decree or free will, and you in this instance, didn't wake up.

When your spouse wakes up (he/she) feels stranded, with no direction and desperately seeking for the first person willing to help. Your spouse is asked if you had left any legal documents pertaining to your death to which is replied, "NO."

Then your spouse is asked if you had any life insurance he or she may know of and again the reply is, "NO." Then your spouse is asked how much money there is between your checking and savings account at which he or she replies, *I don't know!*

Now your spouse must pay in full for your burial expenses. Your inherited assets are transferred to their account, but tagging along are all the appropriate debts that the law stipulates must be paid.

Your spouse's legal expenses are on the rise now that he or she has to go through probate court, and is in desperate need of legal advice for all those unresolved issues you left behind which now need to be taken care of.

Therefore, your spouse's income is limited now; your debts must still be paid and after your burial expenses, your spouse is out $10,000 from your checking and savings account.

Little did you know that in the absence of adequate savings and the shortfall of not having a life insurance policy, now your spouse finds himself or herself entangled in life without resources, and aging will be much harder from now on.

Now you see your spouse desperate for not knowing what to do while seeing himself or herself with no financial security for the years to come. And there is nothing you can do.

And as much as you want to cry out loud about how sorry you are, he or she cannot hear a word you are saying, not because she is ignoring you, and let's remember the words of the homeless man: *Because you need air to speak, understand? You-need-air—without air you cannot be heard!*

Do you see what I've seen over and over again throughout my years in the insurance industry? Take care of your business affairs *now*, so when the time comes you can feel the peace that brings having all the earthly issues resolved.

Think about it! It may not be a legal obligation, but rather it's a moral obligation you owe to those you are leaving behind.

This and many similar cases occur every day on Earth as a result of not having resolved the basic legal and financial issues needed to guard against the troublesome world we live in; and along with it, leaving behind people who depended on us and whom we had agreed to share our lives with in all ways.

If you depart prior to your spouse, it is your moral obligation to clean up your act and business affairs before you leave—it is as simple as that.

My best advice is to get your legal affairs in order for continuance or liquidation. Get a Durable Power of Attorney (DPOA) for health, medical, and financial affairs and create a Trust (*if that applies to you*).

Formalize a will or testament, and most importantly, build a nest egg for you and your spouse, considering that if you leave prematurely, that money will be enough to give you peace of mind knowing you have left adequate resources for your partner to live well on when you are gone.

Think of it: How free you will feel when you know that you have done your best having settled all those issues for those loved ones you are leaving behind?

That's why I was so tranquil when in 2002, I saw *the light*. I knew that if I were to let go, my spouse and children would have been legally and financially set for life. I had no reservations in that aspect of my life, and that is what kept me in peace, even though I chose to return.

I strongly urge you to do the same and do your due diligence regarding what you know must be done since you are now fully informed. Write it down and move on with your new task. But be cautious, because there is a lot of misinformation, deception, and confusion out there, driven by contract fees and sales commissions, as to what's the best alternative for you.

Do not rush. Take refuge in knowledge first before you believe the first word of advice someone may give you, and don't be afraid to search over the internet until there's enough validation that the plan you choose is the most appropriate for you.

Lessons to be learn:

§ Get your legal business affairs in order, as soon as possible.

§ Get your financial business affairs in order, as soon as possible.

My message to you:

Let me give you some words of wisdom I once was given during my early years in the insurance business and now I pass on to you with a twist: *If every spouse had ever known what every widow knows, every spouse would have all their business affairs in order.*

Before reading the next chapter, please put this book down and write a note in your agenda to start working on this and do not, repeat, do not keep postponing what you know needs to be done.

Chapter 9
Lessons To Be Learned

A SPIRITUAL EXPERIENCE, communication or divine intervention is nothing more than a spontaneous contact with the plane of reality that we come from and belong to.

Those who have come back and recall the experience, to then tell their story, must understand that perception plays a significant role when it comes to interpreting the experience lived.

The *other side* still remains a mystery for many, only because it has been depicted in so many ways, given so many interpretations, and tainted with so much imagination, that one story can literally disclaim the other if enough logic and reasoning comes into play.

It is through understanding and reasoning that any given mystery is unlocked:

If there is a world here (*physical*) and there is a world there (*spiritual*) then there *is* life in both worlds.

If life *is* what we experience here (*physical*) and life *is* what we experience there (*spiritual*), then the spiritual (etheric/abstract) world cannot be denied its existence because that's where our true origin lies; *like it or not, believe it or not.*

It's not that you will go to a place as if you were going to move from one country to another; nor is it that you are going to live happily ever after in paradise, as depicted by many.

It's a realm where your mind, which is your soul (*which is you)* will keep experiencing life but with one little detail. You will no longer be carrying your physical body with you, nor will you have the boundaries and limitations of that physical body.

That means that you must learn to control your state of mind, like the toddler who at first, cannot coordinate its movement.

Therefore, let me just give you a some highly-suggested rules to keep you on track, so when the time comes, you can be mentally, spiritually, and emotionally ready for the transition:

Do not fear death: Death is just a transition that takes place when you leave your physical body behind and move to new realms. There you will still be learning, understanding, and through free will or decree, return once again to the physical at some time.

There is an old story that goes like this:

A sage was asked: How long have we been on this journey? And the sage replied, Imagine a mountain three miles wide, three miles high, and three miles long. Once every hundred years, a bird flies over the mountain, holding a silk scarf in its beak, which it brushes across the surface of the mountain. The time it would take for the scarf to wear down the mountain is how long we've been doing this.

Think about it and you will no longer fear death, for you have been doing this for as long as the first movement took form.

Do not mourn the dead: Once you understand how life continues, you should not mourn those who have moved on to the spiritual realm and are very much alive and doing well.

I don't want to imply that you should never mourn a lost loved one, because it is part of being human to feel emotional pain, and you should let yourself grieve as you learn to detach, but, don't get stuck feeling sorry for yourself and *do* move on.

When you persistently mourn the dead, you are doing it to yourself and to them, because they feel and mourn as well seeing you suffering, not advancing, and as such, neither can they.

This concept can be better understood by watching the 1998 film *What Dreams May Come,* featuring the late Robin Williams.

Do not hold onto attachments: This is a tough one to deal with due to having so many variables. The first attachment you must let go of is of your physical life.

No one wants to leave if there is uncertainty as to what lies ahead; but, if it is well understood and accepted that death is just packing your bags to go to new realms, then it shouldn't be as hard.

Detaching also means, letting go of our family members and friends, your belongings, and so much more. A fully detached soul is one who's truth has set him free.

This reminds me of the old days when someone took a plane, a boat, or a train and the departure was full of emotions, tears, and grief.

Society terms it as a blessing because emotions represent love, but when you acquire Higher Truth, you realize it shouldn't be that way.

I don't recommend to anyone to shut off an emotion and pretend to be strong. Rather, understand where the emotion comes from, embrace it, and with even greater love, smile, be content, and be at peace knowing that nothing will change, except the attire that will be left behind.

My advice: *Travel lightly, the less baggage the better!*

Amend, amend, amend: You have no idea how many I have known who, while bedridden, have asked for loved ones to call old adversaries to amend long held resentments for any given wrongdoing; theirs or the others.

Those are the thorns that hurt the most when you know your time is getting close and you may get stuck with a thorn you must let go of.

It is not just from believing you've done no wrongdoing that absolution from erring takes place; it has been written for eons, from books to tablets, and the same message has prevailed as clear as the law of Cause and Effect: *By no means the unjust will go unpunished.* — *(ancient proverb)*

I am hereby not pretending to impose or propose condemnation for any wrongdoing, since I am not here to judge, nor should anyone ever judge; I am just helping you understand that humanity has been incorrectly led to believe that by forgiving themselves from any wrongdoing their soul will automatically be clean for good as in absolution.

In essence, what metaphorically speaking takes place when you forgive or are forgiven is that the bleeding stops but the harm done still needs to be amended.

Amend as much as you can, starting today, for if you don't this will (in the end), be another piece of baggage you will be carrying with you. Trust me, you don't want to pack heavy going to that new place (*metaphorically speaking*), where at first you will not be very familiar with.

Forgive: Forgiveness is the toughest to assimilate due to the many connotations given to this word. The understanding of forgiveness to a Christian is not the understanding of forgiveness to a humanist. Neither is the understanding of forgiveness to the atheist similar to one from the spiritually awakened.

But what I can do is help you better understand forgiveness from what I receive, perceive and transcribe from the *Collective Forces of Knowledge and Wisdom*:

Forgiveness' synonym is not to judge. You forgive not by exonerating someone from his or her act, but from your judgment. To exonerate is not your role—but resentment is what needs to be voided from your soul. —Transcript

By understanding and being true to the law of cause and effect, you suddenly realize that life will rebalance itself and you pay no judgment for their actions as you see life unfolding. —Transcript

By following these basic principles; from not fearing death to forgiveness, you will begin to see life differently. I have seen myself becoming more compassionate, wiser, patient and more confident as to what my purpose is here on Earth in this lifetime. I assure you that if you follow my work, you will find your purpose, too!

As to how much understanding I have of the spirit world; well, because of it I have never felt closer to my mother today, than when she was in the flesh. I do contact her and she contacts me from time to time, and words need not be exchanged to acknowledge the presence of one another. True love is expressed with the expressed intent, which cannot be misinterpreted, as words often are by men.

The most important aspect I want to stress upon, is the fact that when you die, *you-are-going-to-still-be-you!* And as life continues, so does what you have left behind or undone. Life continues, and what you have done wrong, if you haven't amended it in this lifetime, *you* will meet it again *yourself* in the lifetimes that follow.

Now, for those who have had a near-death experience and are seeking answers to their experience I must warn that understanding spirituality is no less complicated than science. From researchers to theorist and from new findings to the latest interpretations it all converges into one thing: *The everlasting search for the truth!*

What I want you to take away from reading this book is that regardless of your religious background, scientific mind or quantum theories you may have heard about, what has been consistent throughout centuries is the existence of a spirit world, regardless of how it has been portrayed.

I've shown you a glimpse at the spirit world and how I brought what I learned back to memory, without theological ties.

I've shown you a glimpse at how perception works and how you can learn, depending on your set of beliefs and how it manifests.

I've shown you a glimpse at how there is divine intervention. Regardless of how you may perceive it—it's still divine intervention.

I've shown you a glimpse at what an Out of Body Experience is; as one of the many manifestations the soul is capable of achieving while expressing itself.

And finally, I've shown you a glimpse at the law of Cause and Effect so you can take care of your business affairs, because you will never know when your time comes.

What I've shown you throughout this book is a glimpse at what lies ahead when it comes to the spirit world. But keep in mind that I have (*metaphorically speaking*) just scratched the surface when it comes to understanding the spirit world.

In my next book titled *NDE, OBE and Spiritual Experiences,* I interviewed, analyzed and assisted those who had seen the spirit world.

These are real people, with real names who had their pictures taken with me after each interview to validate the source. These are people from all walks of life, whom I chose personally.

They are true experiences of those who have encountered the occult, from those who speak to those already departed, to those who can see the past when holding an object or a hand.

Throughout each interview, I gathered evidential facts of near-death, teleportation, astral travel, out of body and spiritual experiences including interviewing those who could channel the spirits, and those who know the spirit world including what I have learned over the years from all modalities known to men.

I also interviewed lifelong psychics, mediums, and those whom I know personally for their integrity and honesty—not their fame. As a caveat, I included a personal interview I did with a *spirit of light,* exclusively for this book, through a medium I personally know.

Now, as far as *this* book is concerned, I have clearly pointed out that perception is what makes one's experience seem different from another, but nevertheless, there is always a common denominator, which is the realization that there is another world that awaits us all— *like it or not; believe it or not.*

Please keep in mind, though, that when the soul returns from an NDE, OBE or spiritual experience it is only what is brought back to memory that can be accounted for. Any experience that may have taken place and the brain cannot yet translate will be left unannounced until you acquire Higher Truth.

Therefore, keep learning and fine-tuning, for when the time comes you may be attuned to understand the new realm at which you will be vibrating.

Let me help you learn Higher Truth one step at a time, as I explain through my writings how to make sense of it all, until we both can finally converge all disciplines into one and then let the truth speak for itself. Let me explain:

We have been conditioned throughout centuries to see the spirit world as something mystical, the product of sorcery, witchcraft, hocus-pocus, black magic and so many other negative connotations that most people actually feel apprehensive when exploring deeper into the spirit world.

See how many true psychics, mediums, clairvoyants, and many other true gifted individuals have been persecuted and tried as evil, banned from society, incarcerated, tortured and murdered by those who claimed *to know* the truth!

And yet today, there are still many in the field of the paranormal who feel safer by keeping to themselves their gifts for fear of persecution.

If you are on a mission to find the underlying truth, there are a few steps I can help direct you to, in order to dip your toes into this already complicated world of spirituality.

Read this synopsis and then I'll break it down in three steps for you to follow:

Don't believe everything that your read. When you start reading, you must first find credibility in the writer(s,) know their background, the source of the information used, learn about the writers' character, beliefs and how much of that truth they actually live day by day.

Once the author(s) prove to be credible in your opinion, then look for their <u>principles</u> and <u>final goal</u>. What is written in between those lines are the elements each uses to drive you to *their* truth.

Your first step is to learn to separate the grain from the shaft, therefore, do not simply blindly believe just because someone tells you they found the answer, including me.

When you read, you are reading from someone else's perspective. Many (not all) come from judgmental minds following a teaching, or findings of their own, based on their experiences, including me.

Therefore, you have to be careful not to be driven to conclusions unless it resonates with you once you weigh it and consider it carefully, and only then can you allow or dismiss it based on your present understanding.

See, for instance, how humanity was first told that the Earth was flat and look what we know now. The masses believed the scholars and no one dared to challenge or question those in authority at that time.

And those who questioned authority were tried for heresy, found guilty and became incarcerated or executed.

Today, there is a different story. Because, now anyone can speak out, using theories from left to right or anywhere in between with the possibility of us becoming more confused than ever before.

At first, it was one against the authority, but today it is *you* against all those claiming to know the truth off the top of their head.

So, who do we trust? This is your second step. You must validate the source through the author's background. Find out what gives authority to their proficiency. See if the author is the real deal or a product of a good marketing strategy.

See if the author is affiliated with any particular religion. See if the author walks the talk in their daily life. Look for those details that make you wonder how honest and reliable the author is.

You can learn more about me and my work by login to my webpage *TheTranscript.org*

Theorizing on how life should be lived is easy, but setting the example is a totally different state, only a few can truly achieve. I have found through the years that there are many who have claimed they were gifted, anointed, and even "touched" by spirits and once success strikes, opulence changes them forever.

Your third and most important step is to find out what is the author's final goal, where is it taking you and if the message is to hold you captive with endless speeches, entertaining you into nothingness?

Keep in mind that everyone has an opinion and it is no secret that demagoguery can go a long way towards convincing others of their truth. That being the case, go forward with what resonates with you and not the romance of the words or speech.

It's not so much as what is said as theoretical truth, but if what it is said resonates with you. Don't go into the rabbit hole just because it's been written or because there's a new theory.

Ask yourself these questions that you need to ask first and get an answer that will help you move forward before jumping to a conclusion just because it makes you feel good.

Each belief system will tell you something different, therefore, making you ask: Who's correct and who's not Let's just take a look at some of the most common belief systems to prove my point:

When we die, one common belief is that we will be in eternal sleep until resurrected.

Another belief is that we will leave the body and then live in spirit forever.

As another belief is that we will live in flesh in another place already waiting for us.

In addition, another belief is that we will become a collective consciousness.

And a further belief is that at death everything ends.

There are also other beliefs not mentioned here due to the limited extent of this topic in this book. So, who is correct and who's not?

These are all claimed to be words from higher sources when you ask each ideology leader (making you wonder who is telling the truth)! Well, as one of the Transcripts read:

Truth is one, interpretations many. —Transcript

Truth is one, interpretations many, simply means that the message is interpreted through the perceptive mind, leading to each individual's own interpretation, based on what they want to convey, including purpose and ultimate goal.

As for the receiver, it means that their interpretation is based on their preconceived ideas, trust in the source, and what best suits each one's ideals.

I've heard of those who today are channelers of higher sources, but each one of them delivering a kind-of-different message. Isn't that confusing? If truth is one, how is it that spirit channelers don't deliver the same message across the nations?

Many channelers have claimed having conversations with God, others claim having contact with those who once had given names while serving as Angels,

Archangels, Saints, Prophets and so on; when in essence, it is just the channeler's perspective providing comfort, trust and association to help them focus on the energy source.

Don't take me wrong. I do respect and acknowledge when someone I've grown to trust tells me he or she communicates with an Angel, Archangel or a character known from deity. It's just that the level of understanding I'm bringing forward needs to be addressed.

In my personal case, I asked for the identity of the source by which the Transcripts come through and I received the following answer:

Name calling limits the source through reasoning; rather call it to come from the Collective Forces of Knowledge and Wisdom. —Transcript

Who to believe, is a study you must do on your own from what I just explained about any given author, writer, blogger, speaker, lecturer, scholar or teacher. And if you want to become an autodidact, as I did in 1979, this is the moment of truth when it comes to learning how.

Let me show you how to become an autodidact, if you are interested in becoming one yourself:

First choose the one topic that you want to take on and study it until it makes sense.

Once focusing on the subject, an array of questions will come up. I suggest you write them down on a series of index cards or a separate pad you can use as they arise.

Tackle each question and look for answers from the source(s) you have chosen and see if it brings up more questions.

Begin to discard the source(s) where you find that the information becomes senseless and as new answers begin to become clearer in your mind.

Keep in mind that few are the true facts, but opinion abounds. Therefore, choose your source wisely.

Soon you will find yourself submerged in a sea of topics. That's why you need to focus in on only one topic at a time.

Becoming a true autodidact takes a lot of discipline and confidence in one self's judgment. Otherwise, you will become a puppet of the latest book you read or ideology you sought.

I've personally lived the experience watching how my father searched for answers by submerging himself in one belief system after the other.

All it took for him to change was reading a new book on the topic to renounce his previous beliefs and embrace a new doctrine.

Ironically, every time he found himself in sync with the latest belief system, he avowed to having found the ultimate truth. Although I could only visit him every other year or so, I listened as he spoke of his latest ideology, but also kept observing from a distance his next move.

This personal experience with my father is the perfect example of what *not* to do. A true autodidact follows the three steps I gave you and makes no judgments of his findings until the whole picture is seen and then some.

Only your own firsthand experience surpasses someone else's writings or speeches and then true judgment can only be formulated once you take the three steps and apply them to yourself.

Chapter 10
The Beginning

THIS BOOK HAS BEEN WRITTEN to help you better understand what a near-death (*spiritual*) experience truly is. I've also shown you a glimpse of the spirit world and what lies ahead. And ultimately, I sincerely hope you've learned how to *pack your bags lightly* for when the time comes.

I have proven myself to you by being true to my words when in the first chapters I told you that none of what I wrote in this book came from what you and I may have read in books, searched over the internet, learned from gurus or masters, taught by secular teachings or read from scriptures from around the world.

All that I wrote here came from firsthand experiences that I lived, experienced and brought back to memory, to help you better understand the spirit world, without theological ties, this time around.

Now, throughout this last chapter I will disclose what I consider to be the beginning of a new journey; making all previous chapters in this book "the chronicles," or the true story behind the Transcripts, if you will.

The year was 2010. It was the third day after I had joined a free meditation class my wife wanted us both to attend. I had always tried unsuccessfully to meditate but my wife was eager to learn. So, we both attended the meditation class and although it felt peaceful, the first session was as futile for me as previous sessions I had attempted in the past.

Then it came to the second session of this class, with similar results. But, when the third session was about to end, with only about five-seconds from the chime bell ending the session, I went into what I could only describe metaphorically as going down a spiral, touching bottom, and an inner voice whispered in my ear the following words:

—From now on, you will no longer learn from outside sources; and moving forward everything is going to be learned from within.

Unaware of exactly what had just happened, and although baffled by the experience, I accepted these words and complied.

Honestly, I had no idea what was I complying with. Neither did I know what it meant, but somehow, I knew it had something to do with my thirst for answers. So I cut all liaisons with my spiritual readings and waited.

Little did I know that what was prophesied in 2010 came to pass on July 7, 2011, when a *spirit of light* manifested through my son's voice to remind me of an agreement that took place in 1979, (at the time of the accident) in return for my life. But first, it answered all those questions I couldn't get a straight answer for from humanity and before closing, I was granted access to Higher Truth so I could finish my quest and begin my work.

My son's words have been transcribed verbatim through what is known as automatic writing, in what, hereafter, will be called, the *First Transcript* for all humanity to read. In 775 words, the *First Transcript* discloses our true nature, origin and purpose of life by means of answering those questions I asked, and for all of us who continue to keep asking.

Its content is simple enough for many to read; yet profound enough for the spiritually versed, but keep in mind that the answers were given to me at an elementary level that I could understand back in those days, with the simplicity that a child could understand.

You may access the *First Transcript* by logging into my website, but I would suggest you finish this book first to avoid you getting distracted by curiosity.

Then you can appreciate its content much better and with more wisdom once you've finished with this book.

As to me personally having access to Higher Truth. It's the fulfillment of an agreement which I made (at the time of the initial accident) to become the conduit by which the information of Higher Truth comes through to me by having the inherent ability to receive, perceive and transcribe the true intent from the *Collective Forces of Knowledge and Wisdom* pertaining to the origin and purpose of life.

Higher Truth allowed me to recall those events, that I rendered in each chapter of this book in order to be able to attest to those spiritual lessons that I couldn't foresee in the past.

Today, Higher Truth allows me to take these accounts as evidential facts, which have been recorded in time and space from a past that cannot be denied, to show the analytical, skillful inquisitive and stubborn fact finding autodidact in me, that what was given, including the 2010 prophesy which came to pass in 2011, were lessons that I had to take before I could finish my quest and begin my work.

As for what is Higher Truth?

Higher Truth is like math!

Do you remember when you first learned to count numbers in school?

I do. I was so young I don't even remember how young I was, but it must have been in first grade. I'll never forget the day the teacher said:

—*Class, today you are going to learn the foundation for all the numbers. You are going to learn how to count from one through ten!*

I was so ready to recite what I thought to be all the numbers. And when I recited them effortlessly in front of the class, I felt as if I had achieved my most successful goal of having memorized all the numbers!

But deception came in the next day when the teacher said:

—*Class, today we are going to learn how to count from ten to twenty.*

I was in shock!

How could it be that I was lied to!

I thought I had just learned all the numbers!

And now I found out there was more to it!?

I was not lied to. I was told the truth. I indeed learned all the numbers. It was just that once I learned all the numbers, the next step was to learn how to combine them in a new set of values, through double digits! Learning to count double digits was learning Higher Truth.

I was told enough truth that I could understand in my early stages of math. I later had to learn Higher Truth while adding and subtracting. Then, Higher Truth when multiplying and dividing, and much Higher Truth when I learned how it all lead me to <u>algebra</u>.

Imagine a teacher telling a first grader the whole truth, as we know it today, in math! Let's see:

—*Class, today you're going to learn, memorize, and quantify an infinite number of combinations in a numeric sequence. Then you are going to learn to break them down by adding, subtracting, multiplying and dividing each set in an infinite number of combinations; including but not limited to positive and negative numbers, fractions and power values, over algebraic formulas, geometry, calculus and trigonometry! And class...if you all behave, I might tease your brain with a bit of numerical quantum physic theories.*

No child's mind would ever be capable of comprehending such a level of Truth taught by a teacher; not even an adult who was never taught math could absorb all those concepts in one term.

You must first learn how to count from one to ten before you can learn how to add and subtract, before you could learn to multiply and divide before you could solve basic Algebraic equations. Learning Higher Truth will give you the wisdom to solve those equations, equated to understanding life in flesh and the soul's quest for its existence.

Higher Truth won't give you the absolute truth, for this concept cannot be fully comprehended by the human mind. It simply takes you one step closer to the absolute truth, which is in each one of us.

This book is an example of having already learned to count from one to ten and today you are learning to add and subtract, but related to steps in the spiritual realm. I might have digressed a bit from the subject while explaining Higher Truth, but let me now continue with the origin of the *First Transcript.*

As to my being granted access to Higher Truth so I can finish my quest and begin my work. Let me explain:

In the following days, I began to wake up in the middle of the night, usually between one and three o'clock. I had an intense urge to write what can only be described as an intent, presented to me in abstract form, that I was entrusted with to translate into words; but, not as a narrator reading a script, but rather, like a soldier in the battlefield reporting live as the events took place and how it felt.

Soon I became wiser and I began to voice record each experience to help myself grasp each concept as I transcribed it into words simultaneously.

That's the reason why most Transcripts are written as if I were talking to you and not as a trans-medium delivering a message.

That is also why no one can interpret what is written in the Transcript other than the transcriber himself, *yours truly, Francisco Valentín..*

Let me expand even further, so you can understand, **if** you are familiar with the psychic world:

I lack many characteristics attributed to becoming a psychic or a medium. I do not communicate directly with spirits, or possess the ability to read a person's energy.

I do however, receive, perceive and transcribe the abstract as it is given to me to explain the origin and purpose of life; lived, experienced and kept in memory, in order to put into words, and later explain to you.

Here is an example as a reference, but not supporting or censuring anyone—the case of the late Edgar Cayce; also known as the Sleeping Prophet.

Edgar Cayce could effortlessly go into a trance and allow spirits, who came forward and identified themselves as *The White Brotherhood*, to manifest through him and speak to humanity.

Edgar Cayce could not recollect later any of the events that took place while in trance. Neither did he acquire wisdom from what he channeled.

He only learned, for the first time, (from his own words spoken) as he read them from *his own readings*, as recorded by his life long secretary, Gladys Davis Turner.

Another example, as a reference, but not supporting or censuring anyone, could be the case of Esther Hicks. She becomes a channeler for a group of entities who have come forward identifying themselves as *Abraham*.

Esther Hicks becomes a trans-medium serving as what she refers herself to be *an interpreter* while the entities manifest through her.

Therefore, she may not necessarily recall in-depth what she speaks at a session, and if she does it is probably at a superficial level.

I do not go into a trance like Edgar Cayce; and neither do I become a trans-medium like Esther Hicks. I do, however, receive the intent in abstract form from those forces who have come forward identifying themselves as *The Collective Forces of Knowledge and Wisdom*.

I transcribe the messages, much like a memory flash that I have to explain in my own words. Once transcribed, all is kept *compartmentalized* between my conscious and subconscious mind, and when I'm asked about a particular Transcript I can explain the content in my own words because the knowledge and wisdom has been kept within me.

Let me give you one particular event that serves as a great example to further explain: After having learned how to gently "step-in" and ask questions to the *Collective Forces of Knowledge and Wisdom*, I asked what should I name what I receive, perceive and transcribe from time to time. No word was ever given.

I simply perceived the image of an old papyrus (that came to my mind) along with a sentiment I can only describe as information from long ago known and forgotten (way before the reminiscence of what has been written and we know about today).

I immediately knew what it meant, and wrote the word *Transcripts.* See how it works?

Since then, I've kept transcribing Higher Truth from the *Collective Forces of Knowledge and Wisdom* as I receive, perceive and pass on to you.

.

Chapter 11
Final Words

Becoming spiritual doesn't mean that you are going to close your eyes, meditate and the next day you will reach ultimate enlightenment.

It takes time, effort, conviction, perseverance and most importantly, commitment not to look back once the transition begins.

As I spoke once on behalf of the *Collective Forces of Knowledge and Wisdom* in a live lecture that I did in 2015 (at the Metaphysical Society of Sun City Center, Florida), the following words came through me without ever being thought of first:

Whomever told you that the spiritual way is an easy way, an easy road, is wrong. Why? Because first you have to dissolve your old self.

I'll never forget the day when for the first time ever, (following my 2011 experience) and after having transformed into a different man, I began to miss my old self, and wanted *him* back.

I was torn between who I was and who I used to be and I had to make a choice.

I knew that by going back, I would regain my old habits and pleasures, which I cherished so much. But, I also knew that by doing so I would have to give up the spiritual path that was entrusted to me.

I knew I had to choose between the life I already knew, with its ups and downs, or the new world I barely knew, with its uncertainties but priceless rewards, and I knew I couldn't have both.

Today, as I write these lines, I look back at who I was and I remember my old self as someone from the past in my life.

I won't say it was easy, for old habits are hard to break, and I still struggle with what I know today opposed to my limitations as I progress.

Just to give you an idea of my struggling, let me write down what I have told my wife many times while embarking on this journey:

If I could do all I know, I wouldn't be here today writing these lines and would have merged into oneness, a long time ago.

When you become spiritual, you feel the transformation right away. You come to realize many things that you didn't notice before. You see life differently, and with it, you begin to change your state of mind.

A true transformation is not simply to do what pleases you now in accordance with what has been written by others and follow those rules to a tee. Rather, it is to work inwardly with what you know is wrong and make amends. That is the hardest thing to do and where most people fail; especially, when having to let go of what you cherish the most.

Let me explain:

I used to love watching boxing matches and martial arts fights as a sport— *not anymore.* What once I saw as an entertaining sport, today I see as barbaric violence fed to people much like the Romans did to the gladiators in their days. Not much has changed since: It's all the same dog with a different collar.

I used to dump in the garbage can over ten pound of daily trash—*not anymore*. Since my spiritual awakening I started composting and recycling. That has left me with a minimal amount of trash, reducing over 90% my footprint on Earth.

I used to be an aggressive driver—*not anymore*. Injustice through traffic upset me. If someone cut the line, I used to become enraged and at times I used all in my power to get even. Today, I avoid as much as possible driving during heavy traffic hours and if do, I bathe myself with patience and follow my spiritual path.

I used to love fishing—*not anymore.* One day I caught a catfish and ran out of bait. Without hesitation, I began gutting the catfish while still alive. As I heard a hissing noise coming out of it, I immediately felt the pain he was having and forced myself to cut its head off to finish its suffering. That day was my last day of fishing, knowing what I know today.

I used to love horror movies—*not anymore*. Becoming spiritual taught me how the mind is the soul and how it is nourished through your senses; in this case, my eyesight. If external forces influence your mind, do you want to feed your mind with terror, anguish, blood, pain and deception?

I used to become impatient and judgmental—*not anymore*. Patience was one of my virtues in my early days; but, life taught me to become more aggressive, thinking it was good because it was rewarding.

Now I understand that I was going backwards instead of forward in my spiritual growth. Today, I've regained most of my patience and have kept a bit of judgmental wisdom to avoid falling prey to the deceiver. I have developed a good dose of balance, I feel.

I used to drink milk everyday—*not anymore.* The day I realized how wrong it was to me that we have been taught and how we all have been manipulated into wrong beliefs, I put a stop to it.

Have you ever paused in your life to realize that we are the only species taught to drink from another animal's bodily fluids?

Make a real pause, and think! From that day moving forward, I have no craving for milk.

I used to love to eat meat—*not anymore*. Knowing what I know today and not committing to change my old ways, is to err.

Not only is one able to stop the transgression and genocide practices against ourselves, at a deeper level, but also one must clean one's soul. If you ever knew what I know, and if once you know, you still eat meat, make this your wake up call.

I have heard excuses of all sorts, and because this book is not about *your* eating habits, I will further explain in one of my short book collection.

As I keep growing in spiritual enlightenment, I feel the pain of those in distress, including animals and plants. I care for the way we have destroyed Earth to almost irreparable conditions during these last 100 years of industrialization.

In short, I am much more aware today of a clearer reality that many don't even think exists, especially those things taken for granted.

Would you consider this to be a boring life? Not so. I enjoy the quietness of the night sitting with my wife and talking about life in a spiritual discussion. I am as playful with my children as I have always been.

I like to cook and have some friends over for an exquisite Vegan cuisine (and have great recipes to share as well.)

I love outdoor living including boating, canoeing, bicycling, hiking, camping, swimming, snorkeling and jogging among many other outdoor sports. I enjoy having friends and family over for family oriented table games.

I also enjoy time with friends while playing a friendly game of billiards, ping pong, or an informal game of baseball, basketball, football, volleyball, tennis, racket ball, dodge ball, bocce and bowling among other recreational sports, but don't ask me to keep the score, because I play just for fun, not to win.

But how could you not keep score if competition is what makes men improve themselves? Wrong! Competition only makes rivalry among men. For someone to become a winner, someone must become a looser. In short, when there's competition someone must become better in that area than the other. This is incorrect thinking among men and the reason why there should only be a time limit or an indiscriminate score for each game.

Sounds boring? Not challenging enough for you? To the contrary! Let me help you better enjoy any given sport, the spiritual way.

When I play ping pong, for instance, I would rather challenge my opponent (whom in this case I prefer to call a partner), to keep the ball in the game for as long as we both can.

The challenge is not to score points, but to make a steady progression for as long as we both can!

Another example is when playing billiards, the fun is to sink the balls through a variety of obstacles in challenging sequences.

When playing baseball, another example, there might be a score to set a time limit to the game, but there is no failure or achievement and the score means nothing to one another except the beginning and end to any given game.

Make your own rule(s) not to challenge your opponent but to entice your partner to share with you a playful game or sport.

Soon you will find yourself helping your partner improve himself and you both will enjoy the thrill of the moment.

As you can see there's nothing boring in becoming spiritual. It's just that once you realize that this world we all live in, has taught us incorrectly, then you begin to make changes, as I did.

The challenge is to better one another so both individuals or both groups could enjoy the best of games and not looking for victory over one another.

See how it works?

When you change your state of mind and how you view things, you will change those who surround you, including your adversaries as you transform them to become your partners instead of competitors.

Becoming spiritual is not as if one day you decide to drop everything, transform yourself overnight and achieve nirvana.

As I just said, *It takes time, effort, conviction, perseverance and, commitment not to look to the past once the transition begins.*

Start with simple things, such as, your next game of cards or sport. Avoid becoming an adversary and turn competition into what you used to when you were a child. Just play as you did before someone taught you to challenge your opponent in exchange for a prize or claiming victory over others.

Now, here is your second challenge: During your spiritual awakening, you will be struggling with temptation. But, let's first define (*) temptation:

(*) Temptation is everything that distracts you from your specific goal with the promise of the pleasure of gain.

If you want to lose weight, food will become temptation. If you want to become spiritual, then temptation is all that holds you back from achieving enlightenment;

including, but not limited to lust, greed, vanity and pride, among other aspects you personally must avoid.

And the battle begins with what you cherish the most, knowing deep inside, that it is not good for your soul.

Here is where denial plays a significant role. Many claim you can keep your old ways and still reach enlightenment, and here is where denial becomes a temptation in itself.

And because I don't want to sound as if I'm preaching to you about a future boring life, I made sure you know from my previous paragraphs all the exciting adventures this *yogi* enjoys along with my busy schedule compared to the sedentary life of many.

Indeed, there are going to be times when you will refrain from doing what once was appealing to you and you will be tempted to give-in, especially with your eating habits and the world famous "cheat day."

Did you know that if you want to change the world, and if in a 7 billion people world, 50% choose, like me, one day not to support the beef industry, the whole industry would collapse overnight?

But if out of those 50% there is a great majority having a "cheat day," you are then indeed supporting the beef industry, therefore losing the battle?

This would also bring a twofold situation, because a "cheat day" will keep holding you back.

In other instances, you will feel nostalgia for the things you no longer do, it will make you doubt, and you may try it one last time. Please don't.

The simple act of experiencing one last time what you no longer do will get implanted in your mind and to shake it off will be a new unnecessary odyssey to embark upon.

That's why you should <u>not</u> go back!

Let me then give you some pointers to help you on your new path, if you choose to walk the spiritual path:

Understand that We Are One: Even those who proclaim oneness seldom understand this overused word. In simple terms, it takes stretching the mind, and still, it is hard to grasp the concept that *all* of us are <u>One</u>.

You may understand it as a concept, but really sinking into such realization is intensely hard to grasp and even harder holding it in your mind.

Even those who proclaim having such intense realization of oneness, often fail to follow these rules I'm about to disclose.

Do not do unto others that which you do not want done unto you: This is a tough one when you examine yourself and see how many times you have done someone wrong, even when you didn't notice it at first and learned later while reviewing your day.

It requires an overwhelming amount of discipline to abstain from transgressing against others. And remember: *Whatever wrong you do to others, you do it to yourself, because we are One.*

Become vegan: Once you realize that you must kill one life to sustain your own life, choose to kill from the lesser (in conscious mind).

This last I learned from the Transcripts, and as I follow the original intent, it hurts as I feel the suffering from those incarnated souls who have been raised in captivity for human consumption.

Once it was written: *Thou shall not kill.*

Now that you know the truth: What are you going to do about it?

That doesn't mean you are going to become a (*) breatharian overnight. You must first change your vibration (state of mind) to change your body chemistry gradually. Otherwise, you might develop health issues.

I myself am in the vegetarian stage while learning to become Vegan. Becoming breatharian is not my immediate goal, although I don't discard it or even know if I will ever achieve it in this lifetime, but I must see where <u>my own path</u> takes me in accordance with reaching <u>my final goal</u>.

(*)Breatharian—a person who subsist healthily on air alone. Only a handful of true breatharians still live today while many attempt or claim attempting but fail.

Note: I do not promote for you to change your diet unless you first learn in depth the spirituality aspect of it. I do, however, recommend for you to become well informed before changing your diet.

Care for and preserve this world for future generations to come: Knowing the karmic law and the evolutionary process of the soul through the act of reincarnation, you don't want to fall victim to your own creation in upcoming lives.

Since you may not want to come back to an eroded and harshly inhabited planet (Earth), do what is right to preserve for others what you have left behind.

Here you will see the law of Cause and Effect in full force, as it has shown us all through history and we are still so blinded that we don't see it, and even when we do, we do little or nothing about it.

I have recently become a grandfather, and it hurts me knowing the world we are leaving to these new souls who are presently incarnating on Earth.

Leave a legacy for the children of your children, and be careful; you may reap the fruits of your own actions in future reincarnations to come.

Amend: Previously posed, this shall become your virtue moving forward—your ability to make amends from previous errors in your life, and do better every day moving forward. It follows *forgiveness*, which is the letting go of resentments. This eventually will begin to mold you to becoming your new self.

Take this book as an introductory piece and keep moving forward seeking Higher Truth. Log on to my webpage *TheTranscript.org* and become part of those seeking the way back home, in a rational way, *without theological ties, this time around.*

You can start by reading the book *NDE,OBE and Spiritual Experiences* to learn more about the spirit world. And if learning spirituality is not on your priority list, then I suggest you read my forthcoming book titled *The Transcript*.

In the latter, you will learn how we all have been taught so incorrectly for eons, as you unravel, with me, the meaning of each spoken word depicted from the *First Transcript.*

This journey of ours, throughout this book, has been just a glimpse at the spirit world. I invite you to become part of those souls who, by changing their ways, are leaving a legacy for others to follow, from spiritual wisdom to saving planet Earth.

Meanwhile, may Peace and Love abound in all of you as it abounded in me while experiencing life, as we know it, in the place one step closer to home.

Thank you for sharing time with me.

—Francisco Valentín
Author and publisher of the Transcripts

TheTranscript.org

Manufactured by Amazon.ca
Acheson, AB